THIRTY-SEVEN

Essays on Life, Wisdom, and Masculinity

By

QUINTUS CURTIUS

THIRTY-SEVEN
Copyright © 2015 by Quintus Curtius

ISBN-13: 978-1502848277
ISBN-10: 1502848279

I did not know how good a man I was till then...and I remember my youth and the feeling that will never come back any more—the feeling that I could last forever, outlast the sea, the earth, and all men; the deceitful feeling that lures us on to joys, to perils, to love, to vain effort—to death; the triumphant conviction of strength, the heat of life in the handful of dust, the glow in the heart that with every year grows dim, grows cold, grows small, and expires—and expires, too soon, too soon—before life itself.

--Joseph Conrad, *Youth: A Narrative*

TABLE OF CONTENTS

AUTHOR'S NOTE

All writing, it has been said, is a form of exhibitionism. Writers can tolerate nearly any indignity except being ignored. Most of the essays in this book were written in basic form in 2013 and 2014; these have been expanded and amplified. Some of the essays (e.g., the prologue, epilogue, and essays 1, 2, 3, 6, 10) appear here for the first time. Besides exhibitionism, writers have other goals. They seek to stimulate, enlighten, explain, cajole, and, perhaps, to act as gadfly. The Italian humanist Giovanni Pontano, in his dialogue *Charon*, has two of his characters make the following exchange:

"Your wisdom shows itself from all sides. But, you pain in the ass, what are you trying to achieve with these things?"

"What I actually did arrive at."

"Which was?"

"That I am a gadfly, and am so seen by everyone." [1]

It would be hard to improve on this observation.

---

[1] Gaisser, J.H. (ed.), *Giovanni Gioviano Pontano: Dialogues*, Harvard: Cambridge Univ. Press (2012), p. 113. Translation is my own.

PROLOGUE

Rubber ice. That was what his brother Michael called it, those dark and mottled patches that dotted the sheet ice covering the pond near their house. It was an odd, counterintuitive phrase. He couldn't quite understand the *rubber* part about it. Why rubber? Was it flexible? *No*, said Michael sternly, holding him by the cuffs of his pea-jacket and looking at him disapprovingly. *It's called that because it's got no strength. It gives way. So don't ever go on it, you understand me?* He had nodded his head, as he always did when Michael gave him a lecture, knowing that his compliance with instruction would be decidedly situation-dependent. It wasn't exactly that he didn't *believe* his brother; it was just that he had to see, feel, and touch things for himself before he could calculate whether an admonition was worth following. It cannot be otherwise, when one is fifteen years old. It was like that when Michael had told him not to swim out past the barnacle-encrusted rock near the shoreline at the beach they went to every summer. What was the word he had used? *Undertow*, he remembered. That was it. But he had swum out past the rock anyway and never felt any *undertow*.

In the town's city hall, there had been an announcement that bags of coal were to be trucked in starting in late December. The deliveries would continue as demand required for the remainder of the winter. These great seventy-five pound bags were a dirty, clumsy load to handle; the job of handling them fell to those unfortunate enough to be unable to delegate the task themselves. So the chore of transporting several bags to his family's house near Revere Street fell on the capable shoulders of the boy, who relished the importance of his appointment for the job by his father. It was about two and a half miles in total from town hall to his house. He brought with him a sturdy sled with wide steel runners, with a thin five-foot rope attached to the front. The boy had always been surprised at how much weight could be dragged with the sled, as long as the load was balanced and he had a secure grip on the rope. On this day, he had walked over to Town Hall from his house with the empty sled, loaded the bag of coal, and pondered the matter for a moment. He thought he would take a shortcut across the harbor ice on his way back home. It was not a decision he thought long about. It was late January, and Massachusetts winters then were colder than they are now. Regular freezings of the harbor ice were not exactly frequent, but they did happen, and the boy had heard from a few of his friends that the ice was safe to walk on. His brother had disagreed. *Hey. Rubber ice out there, you know that?* This he had said meditatively to the boy, while chewing slowly on a morsel of salt pork during last Wednesday's supper. His eyes had locked for a moment on those of his younger brother, almost challenging him to contradict the statement. But the boy thought the better of it and had said nothing, remembering how such exchanges usually ended.

The boy pulled the coal-laden sled up to the edge of the shoreline and gazed across the surface of the ice. Dried cattails and mounds of crushed reeds poked here and there from the crusty shoreline. He paused for a moment, enjoying the stillness of this frigid expanse of flatness, watching the gentle swirlings of his chilled breath float away from his pursed lips to dissolve into the winter air. With the assistance of optical trickery and the foolishness of youth, to the boy it just did not *seem* far across the ice. Although some patches were covered unevenly with snow, from where he stood the ice appeared as sturdy and as permanent as a sheet of quarried marble. On the horizon, the sunlight reflected off the white and grey outlines of distant houses and the occasional ship's rigging with incandescent steadiness, pulsing in waves of shimmering insistence. He tested the ice on the shoreline and was relieved to find it to be like walking on iron. His plan was to move quickly across the ice, pulling the sled behind him at a distance of about five feet; and on the ice its steel runners made it seem like no weight at all. He had moved about five hundred feet from the shoreline when he began to be conscious of air pockets trapped beneath the surface ice; the pockets squeaked, squelched, and crackled as he moved over them, distributing itself with gaseous regularity in proportion to the weight he applied over it. And then he became aware, slowly, of a change in the quality of the harbor ice. It began to take on a darker hue, popping and crackling ominously as he moved himself and his coal sled over it. He paused before one dark patch as the crackling sounds gathered in an alarming crescendo, and he hastily tried to retrace his steps, when suddenly a gulf opened up in front of him and to his right.

It happened so quickly that he had no time for any preventive measure. Before he could unloop the sled's rope from his clenched mitten, and before he could raise his hands to steady himself or reach out for the ledge of ice in front of him, he dropped heavily into the slushy salt water. The sled crashed into the water behind him, going straight to the bottom and ripping off the mitten in his right hand. The sled's metal runner somehow glanced his exposed wrist and opened up an incision that the salt water instantly made him aware of. His chin slammed down on a large piece of ice has he plunged into the water, leaving another deep cut running from his jawline to his upper lip.

But the worst feeling of all was the shock of hitting the water. There was just no way to describe it to someone who had not experienced it. His entire upper body drew taught and immobile as his muscle fibers contracted with the shock of the extreme cold. It was as if some giant icy hand had seized him and was slowly crushing him in its palm. Breathing became difficult; in place of regular, oxygenating respiration, there was only the great gasp of shock and wooden immobility. His boots, which had taken so long to lace before he had left his house, then began to fill slowly with water; it was a terrible sensation to feel the freezing water trickling around his feet, adding immense weight to the paralysis brought on by the cold.

He desperately fought to reach the edge of the ice sheet and crawl back onto it. His hand was bleeding, as well as his chin, and he could feel an icy sluggishness beginning to cripple his mobility. But every time he clutched the edge of the ice, he could not bring his lower body over the lip of the ice. He lost two fingernails as he groped feebly at the ice lip, and his boots were getting progressively more heavy.

There was not much time; his strength and will were ebbing quickly. But every time he would secure a hold on the ice, a chunk of the ice shelf would break off as he tried to swing his legs up onto it. Fortunately, some air had become trapped in his thick pea-jacket when he fell into the water, and this helped stabilize him and keep him afloat for longer than otherwise might have been possible. In one last great effort, he threw his left shoulder up onto the ice shelf as far as he could. Blood leeched slowly from his jawline onto the surface of the salty ice. He then was able to elevate his lower body to a position where his waist was nearly on the ice; and from there, he made slow, wriggling, back-and-forth movements to shake his legs from the water. With a combination of progressive shoulder-extending and leg-wriggling, he was finally able to leverage himself into a position where he could kick furiously to bring his leaden boots out of the water. It was utterly exhausting, and the muscles of his upper body seemed to be seized up with some kind of musculo-electrical paralysis that he could not understand.

And then he was out of the water, lying on his stomach on the surface of the ice, gasping for air in short, desperate breaths, not daring to make any sudden movements lest new fissures open up beneath him. He could not feel his legs below his knees, and his hands were by now insensate lumps of flesh and bone; and there was no salt-water sting from the gashes on his hands and chin, because those extremities had lost all feeling as well. He rolled slowly—very slowly—away from the hole in the ice, making snowy revolutions over the frozen surface, until he was about fifteen feet from it, and lay there, breathless and exhausted. But he was losing sensation quickly, and he knew that unless he got up and got moving, he would not last long. Each boot was filled with water, and he knew that even if he were able to take them off, he would be unable to get them back on again.

Their heavy metal clasps required a degree of motor skill and dexterity which he no longer possessed. He could barely move his hands. He was trembling uncontrollably and was beginning to feel disoriented. With great effort he stood up, and was able to make out the shoreline in the direction of home, which he identified by the black-and-white spire of the Church of the Nativity near Monroe Street. He stumbled onwards towards the shoreline, driven now more by instinct than conscious effort; as he ran, drops of blood leaked down his chin and congealed periodically on the front of his crusty pea-jacket. Every step was agony; with each step, his frozen feet felt impaled by a thousand needles, as the frozen nerve endings tried to assert control over his limbs.

As his battered frame reached the shoreline, he knew he would need to run the remainder of the way if he were to get his circulation going again. He had passed the beach when he tripped on a cluster of rocks and collapsed in a heap within twenty-five feet of Carnoustie Street. He had begun to drift out of consciousness when two passers-by spotted his haggard shape and lurching frame. Shocked by the gashes on his chin and hand, and by his involuntary shivering and mumbled speech, they carried him to a nearby convenience store, and from there his family was called. It was nearly sundown; if only one more hour had passed, no one would have seen him, and he might have died of exposure. And so, by such slender threads of spider-silk, over churning cauldrons, are our fates suspended.

1. How A Wise Man Should Reveal His Opinions

It is often asked whether one should openly profess one's opinions in an unfriendly environment, or if it is a wiser course of action to remain silent. There is little to be gained from shouting slogans at a prison camp commandant if you are a prisoner; but most situations in life are more subtle and nuanced than this, and require a degree of finesse and dexterity. One is reminded of the doctrine of *taqiyya*[2] in Shia Islam, which permits religious dissimulation as a means of protecting oneself from persecution in a hostile environment. And no doubt this doctrine has had its uses now and then, down through the centuries.

It is in the history of thought that the question becomes most urgent. Here we see that visionary thinkers have, far more often than not, been subjected to the cruelest calumnies and abuses when their ideas have run counter to established orthodoxy. So Copernicus waited until he was safely dead to publish *De revolutionibus orbium coelestium (On the Revolutions of the Heavenly Spheres)*; so Spinoza could not speak openly of his views to his religious kinsmen in Holland; and so Leibniz, remembering Spinoza dying alone in an attic, adopted enough protective coloration so as not to be seen offending the rules of the day. Those whose ideas upset the prevailing belief system

---

[2]The Arabic word is تقية.

should not expect garlands to be thrown their way. Quite different treatment will be meted out. Nevertheless, it is still possible for the adroit thinker to make his points known in such a way that orthodoxy is not unduly alerted.

Consider the case of the philosopher Averröes. Known in Islam as Abu al-Walid Muhammad ibn Rushd, he came from a privileged family in Muslim Spain; his father made sure he received the best instruction available, but his son helped considerably by being a genius. In his day he was most prominent as a jurist and as a physician; he became a judge (*qadi*) in Seville in 1169, and three years later was appointed to a similar position in Cordova. His treatise on medicine became an authoritative text in Western Europe for several generations. In those days it was still possible for a learned man to master several different fields.

When the Islamic authorities began casting around for someone to write commentaries on Aristotle for instruction in the universities, Averröes's name was put forward, and he fell to the task with characteristic intensity. His plan was to write, for each major Aristotelian work, a summary, then a commentary, and then finally an even more detailed commentary for use by advanced students. Like his contemporaries (and us today), he was concerned with the proper relationship between religion and science: could they be harmonized? If so, under what conditions? And should one be dominant over the other?

A wise man, he held, would understand that the stories, fables, and legends of the holy books (of Islam, Christianity, and Judaism) are not to be taken literally. They were needed for the moral and ethical instruction of the people, and so it would be both cruel and unwise to attack the cherished faith of the common man. If we interpret the teachings of religious texts metaphorically, allegorically, or symbolically, we can easily find them to square with the observations made by scientists and scholars. A proposition could at the same time be "true" according to science, but "not true" according to religion, and vice versa: in other words, both science and religion had their own parallel and separate tests for a proposition's veracity. The best state of affairs, he believed, was a situation that (much later) informally existed during the Italian Renaissance: learned men would not be persecuted for incorrect opinions, as long as they made no strenuous public efforts to subvert the established faiths. It was a gentlemen's truce, frequently broken, but having some merit nonetheless.

Above all, Averröes was a rationalist. He had learned something from his predecessor Ibn Bajja (known in the West as Avempace), who, in his *Guide to the Solitary*, had proposed to bifurcate human intellect into the "material intellect" (thought connected to the corporeal body), and the "active intellect" (man's participation in the grander and all-controlling Cosmic Mind, which governed all living things). We feel the strong influence of Neoplatonism in this doctrine, and can equate Ibn Bajja's "Cosmic Mind" to the "World Soul" of Plotinus. Neoplatonism was already an essential part of medieval Arabic philosophy, and Ibn Bajja in this respect was bound by tradition.

Averröes, knowing his opinions ran counter to Islamic orthodoxy, was careful to adopt protective coloration in professions of piety which filled his writings. But his real opinions are revealed in his commentaries on Aristotle, which were meant only for the most advanced students. Motion, he said, is "linked to time", and without it there can be no time. There has always been motion in the universe, and therefore there was no divine creation of the universe. It has always existed, and it will never end. God exists, but as a vague sort of referee, hesitant to blow his whistle, imposing a weak degree of control over the universe. The "active intellect" (restating Ibn Bajja) permeates the bodies of all men, and is the same for all; it alone animates him, and gives his body contact with immortality. For the active intellect alone is immortal, and man's highest purpose should be to achieve some degree of union with this cosmic mind; achieving this can elevate

14

man to godlike status. Although these views share much in common with the Neoplatonist tradition, Averröes believed that union with the active intellect could better be reached by rational thought and contemplative wisdom, rather than through the intoxicating ecstasies of the mystic. Perhaps it is only a matter of style and personal taste. Averröes's supreme pleasure was that of the scholar at home in the reflective quietude of his study, while a die-hard mystic pantheist like Ibn Arabi found the same satisfaction in his inspired flights of imagination. There is more than one way to achieve a worthy goal.

Averröes was not popular in the Islamic world. His doctrines owed much to the Greek philosophical tradition that predated Islam; and he felt no need to cater to the religious prejudices of his time. Just the opposite, in fact: he went out of his way to refute the theologian Al Ghazali in his *Incoherence of the Incoherence*[3], thereby earning him the ire of the establishment. He was immensely influential in Christian Europe in the Middle Ages, and his philosophical works, translated into Latin, caused a major crisis of belief among learned men in Christendom. "Averröism" was a dirty word among orthodox religious circles, a term of abuse hurled at those who believed in rationalism over theological faith. Most disturbing were his divisions of "truth" into separate spheres of "theological truth" and "rational truth".

This implied the limitations of faith and the prerogatives of reason; and medieval man did not want to hear that faith had its limits, and was circumscribed by boundaries. Averröes's books were suppressed by the secular authorities of his day. The caliph at Baghdad ordered his writings destroyed in 1150, and this edict was reissued by authorities in Seville in 1194. Most of his important writings were preserved only in Latin translation from the original Arabic; learned Jews translated some of his books into

---

[3] تهافت التهافت

Hebrew, and thereby preserved additional Averröist legacies. In the universities of Paris and London, the debate over Averröism spread like wildfire in the Middle Ages, and stimulated the philosophic output of Roger Bacon, Thomas Aquinas, and countless others. But this debate was never really held in Islam. Speculative thought hid in fear from persecution, and retreated from the sunlight.

A similar lesson can be observed from the life of the German philosopher and scientist Gottfried Wilhelm von Leibniz.[4] A polymath and man of the world who corresponded with the great intellects of his day, he had to take care to cloak himself in the robes of religious orthodoxy to avoid the fate of his attic-bound predecessor Spinoza. Because he was a just and reasonable man, he assumed others to be similarly disposed; and because his keen insight penetrated deeply beneath the surfaces of things, he could never bring himself to accept that Catholics and Protestants would let trivial theological differences destroy the religious unity of Europe. He was a good European two hundred years before the concept became fashionable. Leibniz found his optimism crushed by the realities of power politics. He hoped that the Catholic Church might soften the stance it had taken at the Council of Trent, where it had branded all Protestants as heretics. He corresponded with the influential bishop Jacques-Benigne Bossuet in efforts to achieve the reunion of Christendom from its schism between Protestants and Catholics, and made efforts to have the Church sanctions against Galileo and Copernicus lifted. But it was to no avail. Like his predecessor Erasmus, he was a scholar caught between two extremes, and crushed in the middle.

The Church refused to be moved. France's Louis XIV hammered home the point by revoking the Edict of Nantes and waging years of destructive and futile war against Protestantism.

---

[4] 1646-1716.

To his dismay, Leibniz found Protestants just as bigoted as Catholics; no reconciliation could be had between the rival houses of Lutherans and Calvinists either. He eventually withdrew in bitterness from theology and politics, convinced that scientific inquiry would provide a more useful, or neutral, outlet for his genius. But even there, he was careful to dance around his implications of his views. His doctrine of "monads" logically led to conclusions that would not have been accepted by many of his peers; so he felt it necessary to obscure his true beliefs in a cloud of contradictory and inconsistent statements. He was an optimist by nature, a good man trapped in an intolerant and unreasonable age.

Other thinkers have made no efforts to conceal their doctrines. There is a refreshing charm in openness and sincerity that can disarm even the most strident opponent. Few who have read St. Augustine's *Confessions* can fail to be moved by its utter honesty, passion, and directness; in page after page, he lays open for all the world the migration of his soul from ignorance to enlightenment, using a simple and direct Latin prose style that contrasts favorably with the obscurantism of his pagan peers. Who but one totally at peace with himself could write the following lines from his other masterpiece, the *City of God*?

> This I know, that no one has ever died who had not been
> about to die at some time. The end of life is the same
> whether it makes for a short life or a long one...And
> what separates the situation, in which type of death this
> life may be ended, when the man whose life is ended is
> not forced to die again?[5]

---

[5] Augustine, *De Civitate Dei*, I.11 (Hoc scio, neminem fuisse mortuum qui non fuerat aliquando moriturus. Finis autem vitae tam longam quam brevem

Then again, Augustine could afford to be honest. He was a bishop at a time when Christianity was on the ascendance amidst the death-throes of the classical world. Candor for him carried with it no fear of persecution, unlike the experiences of Averroes and Leibniz. We are confined on all sides by the limitations of time, place, language, and prevailing orthodoxy; he who learns best how to navigate these limitations is most likely to keep his reputation and his sanity. Freedom of speech—something taken for granted today—is a privilege of recent date.

In 1559 Pope Paul IV published the first *Index auctorum et librorum prohibitorum*, the first Index of prohibited writings. Sixty-one printers and publishers were immediately banned. All writings thereafter had to carry the ecclesiastical "imprimatur" or else were outside the law. In Rome, Bologna, Naples, Milan, and Florence, book burnings were conducted which consumed thousands of volumes. One historian tells us that 10,000 were destroyed in Venice in one day. Although the *Index* was revised and somewhat softened in 1564, its presence undoubtedly contributed to the intellectual and scientific decline of Catholic countries after 1600.

In England, freedom of the press found an eloquent voice. In 1644, a blustering cleric proposed that writer John Milton's treatise on divorce should be publicly burned. Parliament had earlier ruled (1643) that all books and pamphlets published in England first be approved and registered with the Stationers' Company, which was essentially supposed to act as a censor. Violations of the law were to be punished with arrest of author and printer.

---

vitam hoc idem facit…Quid autem interest, quo mortis genere vita ista fini-atur, quando ille cui finitur iterum mori non cogitur?)

Milton had never registered his work, and doubtless believed that a thriving intellectual life could not exist in such a restrictive climate. In 1643, he published *Areopagitica: A Speech of Mr. John Milton for the Liberty of Unlicensed Printing, to the Parliament of England*. Milton eloquently argued that the censorship ordinance would produce "the discouragement of all learning…by hindering and cropping the discovery that might be yet further made both in religious and civil wisdom." He went on to say the following:

> Who kills a man kills a reasonable creature, God's image; but he who destroys a good book, kills reason itself, kills the image of God, as it were in the eye. Many a man lives a burden to the earth; but a good book is the precious life-blood of a master spirit, embalmed and treasured up on purpose to a life beyond life…We should be wary therefore what persecution we raise against the living labors of public men, how we spill that seasoned life of man preserved and stored up on books; since we see a kind of homicide may be thus committed, sometimes a martyrdom, and if it extend to the whole impression, a kind of massacre; whereof the execution ends not in the slaying of an elemental life, but strikes at that ethereal and fifth essence, the breath of reason itself, slays an immortality rather than a life.

Milton's words were progressive in their day, but it must be remembered that even he himself advocated censorship of some writings (e.g., Catholic, atheist, immoral, etc.) he considered to have the potential for socially pernicious effect.

New ideas that contradict the established ways of thinking cannot expect to be welcomed with open arms. Those who parrot the party line of the day, who genuflect before the altars of the established orthodoxy, can expect accolades from the mob and praise from those who control the levers of power. It has always been so. Toadies get their crumbs from the master's table. But those who contradict the sacred premises *du jour* can expect very different treatment. The wise man will take care to conceal his unorthodox opinions from the unlettered masses, who have neither the time nor the inclination for speculative thought. Despite all this, perhaps there is something to be said for blunt candor; some men are not psychologically disposed to keep their thoughts bottled inside, and feel an inner need to confront authority. Self-repression eventually poisons the soul. And sometimes trumpeting one's beliefs from the rooftops will do more good than harm. Dissemination can itself become an effective method of concealment.

The experience of Averröes teaches us that the learned man can only rely on other similarly positioned men to confide in; others are neither worthy nor deserving of illuminative revelation. When new ideas are presented, it is better to reveal them in such a way that they are accessible only to those who are deserving of them. So Averröes confined his speculations to Aristotelian commentaries that few would be able to access; and so the learned men of the Renaissance and Reformation were careful to write their treatises safely in Latin, so that they could be understood only by other equals. Today, this failure to filter and screen revelatory knowledge from the unlettered mob is an occasional cause of popular distress. Too many people with inadequate comprehension feel the need to comment on things they know little about. Many of us are simply are ill-equipped to deal with knowledge. The wise man will adapt his methods—but not his convictions—to the circumstances of his time and place, in such a way that he may express his thoughts without endangering his neck. Finding this balance between personal safety and expression remains one of the life's great challenges. The great scientist and philosopher Anaxagoras was exiled from Athens for his daring inquiries into the nature of things which threatened the inherited mantras of his day and, by extension, the temporal powers ruling the city. Pericles did his best to protect him, but it was to no avail. He was eventually forced out of Athens. When, living near the remote Hellespont, he learned that the Athenians had condemned him to death, he replied, "Nature has long since condemned both them and me."

It is the saddest line in the history of philosophy.

2. ON BARBARISM

One of Jack London's favorite themes was the savagery
lurking just beneath the surface of man and Nature. His short story
In A Far County is an unsettling tale about the slow degeneration
of two "civilized" men who decide to spend a winter in an isolated
cabin in the far North. Things seem to go well for them at first,
but then a gradual process of mental and physical deterioration
sets in, caused by their innate laziness, the brutal climate, and a
psychological factor which London calls the "Fear of the North":

> To all this was added a new trouble -- the Fear of the
> North. This Fear was the joint child of the Great Cold
> and the Great Silence, and was born in the darkness of
> December, when the sun dipped below the southern
> horizon for good. It affected them according to their
> natures. Weatherbee fell prey to the grosser
> superstitions, and did his best to resurrect the spirits
> which slept in the forgotten graves. It was a fascinating
> thing, and in his dreams they came to him from out of
> the cold, and snuggled into his blankets, and told him of
> their toils and troubles ere they died. He shrank away
> from the clammy contact as they drew closer and twined
> their frozen limbs about him, and when they whispered
> in his ear of things to come, the cabin rang with his
> frightened shrieks.

The two men act more and more erratically; they begin to
hoard sugar and other provisions from each other, and finally
degenerate into open warfare. A man going to pieces is not a

pretty sight, London knew all too well. He explored the same theme in *Love Of Life*, a grisly tale of a battle between a starving man and a starving wolf, each waiting for the other to die first as they limp across a frozen landscape. Isolation and hardship are the catalysts of barbarism here; they strip away the veneer of civilization and expose the gruesome reality underneath. A recent Russian film, the 2010 drama *How I Ended This Summer*, portrayed the compelling reality of this theme in an effective way. Two men manning a lonely Arctic weather station begin to display passive-aggressive behavior towards one another, and each man believes the other is in the wrong. Minor personality conflicts, unmediated or relieved by contact with others, escalate into major disputes, with disturbing results. Fine manners degenerate into barbaric conduct in the blink of an eye. It is a chilling metaphor for the easy perishability of civilization. Scratch away the surface façade, and the picture of a beast emerges.

What is so remarkable about civilization is how perishable it is. Although it has graced the world for many thousands of years in myriad forms, that presence has not been continuous. Civilization has risen and fallen cyclically, when looked at over a long enough timeline; like a systole and diastole of rise and fall, it has blossomed and crumbled with regularity. As difficult as it is to coax the smoldering embers of civilization into a crackling fire, that same fire can be snuffed out with depressing ease, due to man's baser instincts bubbling beneath his placid smile. I remember hearing a story many years ago which illustrates this point with a devastating certitude.

In May 1829, a seal hunter named Basile Giasson was sailing near Anticosti Island, in the mouth of the Canada's St. Lawrence River. As he was running low on provisions and water, he decided to stop at the island for a day or two in order to resupply himself. Sometime later, he noticed a derelict craft near the shore, apparently abandoned; wondering if he could secure supplies from any islanders, he and several armed crewmen went ashore. Some bloodstained clothing was found near the beach, and there were signs of habitation here and there, but there appeared to be no one close by. There was a small house located a short walk inland, and the four men advanced on it cautiously with weapons at the ready. Inside the house they were confronted by a ghastly and sickening sight: dismembered and preserved human limbs were strung up from the ceiling, dangling nearly everywhere as the men walked about. The putrid odor of rotting flesh hung in the air, mixed with the briny tang of salt and smoke. As they moved into other rooms in the house, they found huge iron kettles filled with human remains and water, as well as wooden trunks containing human fragments packed with salt. Finally, in one room, they found a human figure apparently asleep in a hammock; he had an imposing physique, very muscular, and appeared to be of mixed Caucasian-African ancestry, but he could tell no tale, having been dead for some time.

A short search of the grounds around the house revealed more human body parts, carefully preserved in salt and secreted in bags or outhouses near the main house. The entire spectacle was so overwhelming for the men that they needed to stop now and then to collect their nerves. The rotting condition of the human remains on the grounds, and its attendant horrors, meant that the men could not proceed further until all was buried; they estimated that approximately twenty-four bodies were there in total. A more thorough search of the house the next day yielded further clues. The huge man found in the hammock was named Harrington, and he was from Liverpool; by some stroke of good luck a ship's log was found from an Irish vessel called the *Granicus*, and its entries by Harrington told a ghastly tale of shipwreck, murder, and cannibalism. The barque *Granicus* had left Quebec on October 29, 1828, bound for County Cork with a load of lumber. The vessel had encountered rough waters and been wrecked on Anticosti Island, with all passengers reaching shore unharmed. The house near the shoreline had been long abandoned, however, and there was no food to be found. The twenty five survivors had managed to stay alive by a disciplined regimen of food allocation, but stores were beginning to run short. Quebec in those days was a vast wilderness, and it was not easy for shipwrecked survivors to be found by search teams in that pre-electronic age. At some point, Harrington had murdered the other survivors in their sleep on night, believing that starvation for all of them was inevitable. He went about methodically preserving the body parts of his victims, and actually subsisted for several months on this gruesome diet. The ship's log entries make it clear that he began to suffer from some sort of progressive sickness around March 1829; it is not clear whether this was due to malnutrition or to poisoning by consuming the rotting flesh of his shipmates. In any case, Harrington must have gone insane from a combination of isolation in the cold vastness of Anticosti, and desperation brought about by the fear of approaching death. He had been unable to restrain the beast within, and it had burst forth with terrifying lethality.

Barbarism will always accompany us because it is the original condition of human nature. It is the human default setting. It has its attractions. The refinements of culture involve effort, discipline, and sustained application of will; far easier is it to lounge about and take life as it happens, to abandon oneself to instinct. The historian Tacitus described the Germans of his day, who at that time were barbarian tribes:

> When they are not at war, many are occupied in hunting, and many in leisure, given over to eating and sleeping. The best and most brave of their fighters do nothing, having delegated house, hearth, and field to women, old men, and the most infirm of their families. They relax and enjoy time, by a unique flexibility of personality, as the same men both love inertia and hate quiet.[6]

---

[6] Quotiens bella non ineunt, multum venatibus, plus per otium transigunt, dediti somno ciboque, fortissimus quisque ac bellicosissimus nihil agens, delegate domus et penatium et agrorum cura feminis senibusque et infirmissimo cuique ex familia: ipsi hebent mira diversitate naturae, cum idem homines sic ament inertiam et oderint quietem. *Germania*, 15.

Although Tacitus was more interested in criticizing his fellow Romans than in describing the Germans, the point is that barbarism does not tax the intellect. He found it useful to point to the habits and lifestyles of the Germans as a way of contrasting their supposedly simple and honest lifestyle with the degeneracy of his Roman countrymen. So the myth of the simple, noble savage long predates Rousseau. But one doesn't really feel convinced by Tacitus. A patrician like him would have been profoundly miserable among his idealized Germans, wearing animal skins and skulking about the misty forests of the north. The closer one gets to the myth of the noble savage, the more one realizes that it just doesn't hold water. The novelist Herman Melville tried to live among the South Sea islanders, and he just couldn't do it. They were just too removed in time and space, too alien, to primitive. He nearly lost his mind, and had to escape, no matter what the cost. Initially attracted to the perceived charm of the savage, he found the reality of primitive life to be degenerating and ultimately unredeeming. And he was willing to do anything to escape, as he relates in his novel *Typee*: even to throw a boat-hook into a native's face as he was trying to reach the ship that might carry him off.

As one spans the centuries of history, what one notices above all is the perishability of civilization and culture. In the blink of an eye, it can be gone. Civil war, economic stresses and turbulence, warfare, overpopulation, and collapsing educational standards can all push a person or society over the precipice and into the abyss. In the comforts of our modern society, this fact is so easily forgotten. I remember walking around parts of Sarajevo in the year 2000. Even though the war had been over for a few years, one could find building after building pockmarked with machine-gun fire and rocket impacts. The people I dealt with carried with them the scars of conflict: suspicion, hostility against outsiders, sullenness, and a mute resignation to the sufferings of the moment. Elsewhere, driving in the countryside of Bosnia and

Croatia, one could find small towns nearly blasted off the map; the remaining buildings were just shells of masonry, their insides having been either burned or blasted away. Liberal sowing of mines ensured that the former occupants would think twice about returning. And they never did return. We would meet diligent and brave people trying to resettle refugees who had been previously driven out of one area or another. I respected their dedication and humanitarian impulse, but I could not help feeling that their labors were hopeless. When a man is driven out of an area by violence and death, he is unlikely to return. Why would he want to? Locales are repositories of memories, and the ghosts of these memories haunt the landscape of violated places.

When the beast of barbarism roars in one's face, and one has felt its fetid breath, the experience is not forgotten. There is no going back. The *marranos* and *moriscos* expelled from old Spain in the 1490s and 1600s, respectively, and the countless displaced persons from twentieth century conflicts, found temporary exile to be permanent exile. Even if you could go back, you really can't. Memories of the home country remain just that: memories. Barbarism poisons equally the educated, the innocent, and the helpless; and as a final insult, to ensure the permanence of its victory over civilization, it sows its own salt in the earth over which it has trampled, so that nothing might prosper there again.

That barbaric salt in the soil, once sown there, can take generations to remove.

3. ON STOICISM

My first thought after reading Marcus Aurelius's *Meditations* was that it was one of the most depressing books I had ever read. Although it had a masculine grandeur and nobility of sentiment, it also was fatalistic in a way that leaves the reader feeling as if there is no escape from the unending cycles of suffering in the world. Epicureanism and Platonism at least had the wisdom to try to enjoy the brief span of life we have on this earth, but there was something in Stoicism that seemed sterile and barren. I eventually grew to revise this view. Some of Cicero's philosophical works have made me appreciate that Stoicism, while not a philosophy for the masses, attracted the best men everywhere it took root; and it was an honest attempt to impart a moral code to the ruling classes of the ancient world before the advent of Christianity. Its influence was considerable. It was the most far-reaching and influential of the pre-Christian philosophical systems in the West, and it still attracts men today for the masculine resonance and austere grandeur of its precepts.

According to tradition, Stoicism was founded by a Cypriot named Zeno of Citium, who was likely of mixed Semitic (Phoenician) and Greek ethnicity. It is interesting that the Greater Syrian region produced so many philosophers of note in antiquity (e.g., Neoplatonists like Porphyry, Posidonius, Iamblichus, to name a few). Diogenes Laertius, as always, relates many amusing anecdotes about Zeno, which we can believe or disbelieve as we wish: *credat qui vult*. According to the Stoics, the world can be known only through the senses, but human reason can elevate man above his animal cousins. The universe is a vast material creation, and undergoes periodic birth and rebirth, manifestation and destruction, in endless cycles. Predestination was the rule: the things that happen are ordained to happen, and like the Hindus, the Stoics believed that it was folly to interfere with this inescapable reality. All in all, it is a stern, humorless creed. It trusted too much in "nature" and "reason", and encouraged an unhealthy suppression of the natural appetites. Passion excessively restrained can produce evil just as surely as passion unchecked. We eventually tire of its admonitions to be "wise" and "virtuous", and long to sin safely within our means and abilities. Like any philosophic or religious system, there was often a gap between theory and practice among its strongest proponents. Seneca, despite his Stoic pretensions, hardly demonstrated in his own life an adherence to his professed creed. He pursued money and villas furiously, chased the nectar of power by involvement in palace intrigues against Nero, and finally lost all credibility, along with his life.

But what we admire most about Stoicism is that, despite its faults, it attracted the best men everywhere it spread. It was at least an honest attempt to try to explain the inevitability of suffering in the world, and how a man could rise above it. It appealed to men of action—emperors, politicians, and businessmen—because it provided a comprehensive framework for controlling and soothing the turbulence of the natural passions. And if it was fatalistic, we can accept this as a debt to its Oriental origins. Stoicism provided men of action an explanation as to why so often the universe thwarted their ambitions; acceptance of defeat could be made more palatable if it were cloaked in philosophic garb. It is a noble philosophy, and its ethical code still retains its luster, even today.

For me, the best introduction to Stoicism is one of Cicero's lesser known works called *Stoic Paradoxes* (*Paradoxa Stoicorum*). I like Cicero more than Seneca, as he comes across as more sincere and devoted. There is always something slithery about Seneca. His status as a court fixture in Nero's reign and as a collector of country villas undercuts the credibility of his exhortations to lead a simple life. I even prefer Cicero over Epictetus, whose writing strikes me as turgid and dull. Cicero, always the lawyer arguing his case, churned out these little books of philosophy to convince himself that he was following the right path. I find his nagging doubts appealing. He is the man of affairs finally confronted with the reality of his own exile, removal from office, and mortality. Such conditions focus the mind wonderfully. In *Stoic Paradoxes*, he proposes the following "paradoxes", then answers them himself with admirable brevity. I paraphrase those answers here.

1. **That only what is morally noble is good**. To the question, "what is good?", Cicero answers that a good action is an action rightly, honorably, and virtuously done. "Good" is only what is noble and virtuous. The good and happy life is the life of honor and correct living. Pleasure cannot really be counted among good things, since it "removes the mind from its own seat and state (*mentem e sua sede et statu demovet*)."

2. **That the possession of virtue is sufficient for happiness**. He who places all his possessions within himself alone cannot fail to be supremely happy. To those who see the world as a "single city", exile means nothing; to those whose glory cannot fade away, death means nothing; and those who have led an upright life will not be tormented by the memory of their wicked deeds. The good and wise man cannot fail to be happy. A praiseworthy life is not one to flee from. And what is worthy of praise must be considered happy and desirable.

3. **That sins and right actions (*recte facta*) are equal**. Since all virtues are equal to each other, all vices must be equal to one another. Nothing is better than the "good": good deeds are deeds done rightly, and that which is right must be "good." And since virtues are equal, right actions must also be equal. It follows that since sins proceed from vices, all sins must be equal. Whether

something is a large or small transgression, it is still a transgression. Imagine an actor, says Cicero, who mispronounces a syllable in his performance. We notice the "sin" committed, regardless of the fact that it was a minor transgression. And a ship captain who capsizes his ship remains incompetent, regardless whether his cargo was gold bullion or grain.

4. **That every foolish man is insane**. The wise man is fortified by strength of purpose and security of mind. His virtues render him invulnerable to being "taken by storm." A great quote here, echoing the popular fable of the "shipwreck of Simonides," is "nothing belongs to me or to anyone else that can be carried away or plundered or lost."[7] If a wise man is the acme of rationality by his adherence to the masculine virtues, then the converse must also be true: the foolish man is the acme of foolishness. Another great epigram Cicero gives us here: "Therefore a man will not have the rights of the place where he is located if by law he should not be there."[8] This analogy of the "shipwreck" was a popular one, for we find it again and again as a philosophic teaching tool.

Shipwrecks in the ancient world were a common occurrence, and a frequent cause of destitution. The finest rendition of the shipwreck story as a teaching tool is found in the fables of Phaedrus (c. 15 B.C. – A.D. 50), a Roman slave credited with collecting or composing various fables current in his time, and relating them in simple but elegant Latin verses called *senarii* (iambic verse). Much of his material was indebted to Greek sources, chiefly Aesop. His purpose, he says, was twofold: "to

---

[7] *Para. Stoic.* 29. Nihil neque meum est neque cuiusquam quod auferri quod eripi quod amitti potest.

[8] *Para. Stoic.*, 32. Non igitur ubi quisque erit eius loci ius tenebit si ibi eum legibus esse non oportebit.

draw a smile, and to provide prudent counsel for life." In this goal he largely succeeded, for his work was consistently popular through the Middle Ages and the Renaissance. His retelling of the "Shipwreck of Simonides" (*Phaedrus* IV.22) is a masterpiece of terse wisdom:

> The learned man always contains riches within himself.
> Simonides, who wrote beautiful verses, in order to
> More easily ward off poverty,
> Began to travel around the cities of Asia,
> Singing the praises of notables for financial reward.
> Having become wealthy by this type of compensation,
> He wanted to return to his native land by sea
> (He was, they say, born on the island of Chios).
> So he boarded a ship, which broke apart in the middle
> Of the sea, because of its old age, and a horrible storm.
> Some people collected their bags, others their precious
> Things to sustain their lives.
> One curious person said to Simonides:
> "Simonides, you really have nothing for yourself to take?"
> He said, "I already have all of my things with me".
> Then a few swam away, but most perished due
> To the weight of their possessions.
> Then robbers came: they took what each man
> Had recovered, leaving them naked.
> By chance there was an ancient city near, called Clazomenae,
> To which the shipwrecked men made their way.
> Here there happened to be a learned man,
> Who had read the verses of Simonides, and
> Was a great admirer of him from afar, never having met him.

Recognizing Simonides, he received him warmly, adorning him
With clothing, financial support, and family servants.
The other shipwreck victims carried their blank slates,
Begging for food.
Simonides saw them, and spoke: "I said my things were with me.
And what you brought away from the ship is gone."

A man should not waste his time in useless trifles. Those who place the focus of their efforts on foolish pursuits not only exhaust and debase themselves, but they also waste precious time. Education and knowledge can arm you against the vicissitudes of fate, and the overpowering cruelties of life. The pursuits of vanity will fail us in our hour of need; but no matter the environment, the learned man always contains a store of riches within himself. This portable cargo is our salvation. What we carry with us, is truly ours.

5. **Only the wise man is free, and every foolish man is a slave**. How can any man claim to be the master of his soul, the captain of his ship, if he cannot command it? Can he curb his lusts, resist temptations, control his temper, his appetites, and maintain his serenity? He who cannot command himself can hardly hope to command others. He who is always the servant of his desires and passions is not deserving of being called free. I remember Juvenal's line here about greed: "Love of money increases as the money increases."[9]

If freedom really is the ability to live as we want, then is not he who carries out his own will and judgment in virtuous ways the most "free" of all? If a man's behavior is only guided by fear of

---

[9] Crescat amor nummi quantum pecunia crescit. (Juvenal 14.139).

breaking the law, by fear of ill consequences, by anxiety over this or that issue, can he be said to be truly free? He who follows his own lodestar for the sake of his own virtue acts out of neither fear nor inner turmoil. His disposition liberates him. He is thus truly free. Wicked men, by contrast, are slaves to their own broken and abject wills. He is also a slave who is ruled by his woman:

> Or is a man free whose woman gives the orders, who imposes the laws, and prescribes and orders things as she wishes, who can deny nothing she has commanded of him? If she asks, he has to give. If she calls, he must come running. If she throws him out, he must go. If she threatens, he must live in fear. I truly think that such a man is not only a slave but the worst kind of slave...[10]

Neither does greed escape Cicero's scorn. Those who lust after money, he says, will subject themselves to conditions of the most "unjust servitude" *(iniquitatis in serviendo)* to achieve their pecuniary goals. And the office seeker, that man consumed with blind ambition, who lusts after a government position of authority in order to exert control over others: can he be said to be free? But let us not forget fear: fear too can hold us in slavery. When reason is held hostage by fear or irrational desire, there can be no freedom.

6. **That only wisdom is true wealth**. Wealth is measured by the individual; what we consider "wealth" may vary from person to person. Half jokingly, he notes that no man can be considered "rich" who cannot maintain his own army. The nature of wealth is in productive abundance, and true abundance springs from within. Cicero notes approvingly the story of Marcus Curius

---

[10] *Para. Stoic.* 36.

Dentatus, consul in 290 B.C., who defeated the Samnites after forty nine years of war. When a delegation went to see him at his country estate, they found him roasting turnips in his kitchen. He declined their offers of money, saying that he preferred to rule over the owners of gold to owning metallic gold himself. As no amount of money can equal the value of virtue, it follows that he who possesses virtue has the most valuable asset of all. Even if we have to speak of money and ledgers, who can deny that it is not what one makes, but what one keeps, that is of highest importance. The man who has lavish expenditures will have nothing left over for himself after deducting for all his overhead; but he who lives modestly will be able to get by with little:

> The quantity of one's wealth is not determined by his place in the census-register [i.e., by being a large landowner], but by his way of living and his culture. Not to crave money, is money; not to love buying things, is an income. The greatest and most certain of riches is to be content with one's own things.[11]

Virtue, unlike other types of wealth, cannot be taken from us. It is not lost in a fire, shipwreck, or other calamity. It lasts forever, and has the ability to produce its own income and dividends for our lives. The virtuous man will be content with what he has, will not lust after greater and greater riches, and will ask for nothing. But the greedy and covetous man will never be sated with what he has; always on the prowl for more and more, he will expend his energies in a futile quest to quench an unquenchable thirst.

---

[11] Sed non aestimatione census verum victu atque cultu terminatur pecuniae modus. Non esse cupidum pecunia est, non esse emacem vectigal est; contentum vero suis rebus esse maximae sunt certissimaeque divitiae (*Para. Stoic.* 51).

All in all, Cicero's distillation of Stoicism here presents a compelling argument. But much like Confucianism, it asks of man an ideal that is foreign to his nature and proclivities. It is not easy to live by virtue alone. There is something arid in the Stoic proclamation that virtue alone is enough to keep a man happy. It is not. Still, it is hard to find too much fault here. Despite our practical objections to the Stoic way of life, who can deny the truth of its precepts here? Excepting the ethical system formulated by Christ, it remains the noblest code of conduct that a purely philosophical system can be expected to conceive. In the face of the grim reality of life, what other personal code of conduct can so elevate man, and give his existence such dignity?

In the Nelson-Atkins Museum of Art in Kansas City, which I visit frequently, there is a painting by Jan Steen, a Dutch painter who flourished in the early seventeenth century. The painting, entitled *Fantasy Interior with Jan Steen and the Family of Gerrit Schouten* (ca.1659), depicts a charming household scene with various figures in domestic leisure. On the mantelpiece above the fireplace, there is a skeletal bust of Death, not quite looming over the scene, yet unmistakably present in the background. On that bust of the Reaper is inscribed the admonitory motto *Discite mori*: learn to die.[12] It is a fitting tag for an exhausted Central Europe, which had only recently (1648) emerged from the horrors and devastation of the Thirty Years' War. Steen warns us that this world, and the attendant pleasures of our lives, are only transitory. All will eventually dissolve into the receding mists of our imperfect memories. When I read that motto, I thought of Stoicism.

---

[12] We also find the skeleton motif in Petronius's *Satyricon*, during the scene describing Tremalchio's dinner. The figure of a skeleton is visible to the diners. The author cautions us to enjoy the day, and make merry: "O we mortals! All man is nothing. So we shall all be, after Hades carries us off. So let us live, while things may be well." *Satyr*. 34.

4. ON MYTHS

Man cannot live on food and drink alone. He also needs myths to sustain him, to console him in his bereavements, to provide a code to anchor his life, and to impart a sense of meaning to this mortal existence. Snatch away his mythos, rob him of his ideal, and you banish his spirit to a rudderless drifting in life's drama. It is a cruel fate, and one that is far too common. But for some men, the myth is strong. And it is the last thing to die. Take, for example, the case of Sir Thomas Malory. He was an English knight who fought in the Hundred Years War, and in 1445 even briefly served in Parliament. He was living at a time in which the medieval age of chivalry, the age of the knight, was on the wane. Malory had built up his existence and his identity around the idea of knighthood, chivalry, and the centuries-old moral code that went along with it. But returning home to England after his campaigns in France, he found peacetime society unbearable. Here was nothing in his previous experience that he could call his own; and he found his martial skills to be of little value in civilian society.

He couldn't bear it. He writhed and rolled in his peacetime agonies. His way of life was doomed, and he knew it. At this point, he made a startling reversal. Turning his back on is previous life, he plunged into crime. He broke into the home of a man named Hugh Smyth and raped his wife; he extorted a sum of money from another couple; and then he raped Smyth's wife a second time. He committed a long series of thefts, robberies and burglaries, one even from a Cistercian Abbey. His crime spree came to an end when he was caught and thrown into prison. While languishing in the fetid darkness of confinement, Malory managed to write one of the most elegant and transcendent works of early English prose: *The Noble Histories of King Arthur and of Certain of His Knights.* Time has shortened the name of his book to *Le Morte d'Arthur*. Throughout his thick book, Malory implores his countrymen to return to the ideals of King Arthur and his 150 "Knights of the Round Table"; and in the tragic and timeless stories of Tristram, Lancelot, Guinevere and others, he thought he had found an ideal anchor on which to moor his drifting ship. He requires of a knight never to do outrage nor murder...by no means to be cruel, but to give mercy unto him that asketh mercy...and always to do...gentlewomen succor, upon pain of death.

In *Le Morte d'Arthur*, no one ever gets his boots muddy, the skies are always brilliant and clear in Arthur's ethereal realm, and love and war are equally pedestalized. It is about as mythic and idealistic as a writer has ever managed. Because it had to be. Because Malory knew that he, and his myth, were doomed. How can we reconcile the sublime, airy beauty of Malory's book, and its noble language and moral code, with the base reality of his crimes? How could such a man write such a book? Because man is a complicated being. That's why. Complicated, and with many faces, saying different things from different mouths. He can possess the heart of a monster, and the tenderness of a saint, in equal measure. And somehow, each of these voices needs to speak. But he knew his time was running out, and he died in prison in 1471. The colophon of his book is a poignant cry for help:

> I pray you all gentlemen and gentlewomen that readeth this book of Arthur and his knights, from the beginning to the ending, pray for me while I am alive, that God send me good deliverance and when I am dead, I pray you all pray for my soul. For this book was ended the ninth year of the reign of King, Edward the Fourth by Sir Thomas Maleore, knight, as Jesu help him for his great might, as he is the servant of Jesu both day and night.

For a moral code to take root in a society, and to become embedded in the psyche of a people, it must have some supernatural sanction. It must be based, ultimately, on a system of religious belief. Feudalism, for example, was in theory rooted on Christian morals. Man cannot be exhorted to do good by words alone; he must be held in the grip of terror by a religion that promises damnation if he misbehaves. Religion provides the backing to a moral code that rises above man; the myths, fables, and stories of religion are there for a purpose, and that purpose is to impart a moral code that can keep man's baser instincts in check. Our baser instincts were formed in the hunting stages of man's development, over many hundreds of thousands of years. Those instincts—greed, lust, cruelty, individualism—served man well in that stage of development.

But what were once virtues became, under civilization's restrictions and firewalls, vices; society requires refinement, and a level of cooperative, socially responsible behavior. Hence the moral codes of the world's major religions, which have served to control and limit man's antisocial urges which still pulse and throb in his veins. It follows from this that when religion fades as a source of instruction in society, social morals decay along with it. No one has found an adequate substitute for religion as a source for instruction of youth, for consolation of the old, and for solace to the stricken. Myths are the quintessence of such teachings, cloaked in the charm and digestibility of narrative.

Several years ago I visited the Tower of London. There is a part of the fortress where visitors can look at the wretched cells where prisoners were housed. I remember seeing an attendant on duty there, a pale, grey-haired man sitting at a desk, fidgeting obsessively with a cigarette lighter. The other tourists had left the room, and he was looking out the window. I decided to give him something to do, and began to make idle conversation.

"The carvings on the cell walls" I said, "are amazing. It's hard to believe they were allowed to make graffiti like that."

"Well, now," he began, clearing his throat and shifting himself creakingly his chair, "you have to remember that these inmates were rich people, noblemen and such. They had their knives and tools. Wasn't much in the way of security in those days."

"Yes." I nodded in agreement, anticipating a yarn.

"Here, let me show you something." He walked over to one of the cells and pointed to an amazingly detailed carving in the wall, made by a prisoner centuries before. It was now covered with a clear plastic shield to protect it from the curious fingers of tourists. It looked like a coat of arms, or some family or clan monogram.

I tried to imagine the effort the condemned man must have exerted to produce it, the sustained willpower that would have been required. To carry it off would have required the conviction, or desperation, of a true believer. It may have been the last thing he ever did. His family coat of arms, his lineage, his house, his identity: scratched out in stone for eternity. There it was. His last and final act.

"I can only imagine the effort it must have taken," I said, not knowing what else to say.

"Of course. But it was his identity. In those days, men drew their identity from their family, clan, or spiritual affiliations. They were rooted in tradition, in a way that we moderns are not. We all need something to keep us going, you know." Then he shrugged his sunken shoulders and walked away.

And I thought to myself, *the myth is the last thing to die. When that goes, so goes the man.*

5. THE FATE OF BOETHIUS

My grandfather used to have a phrase he would use when confronted with a situation that only wisdom and experience could fully explain. *The world will teach you,* he would say. At the time, I always saw this as a frustrating response. It seemed so trite, so smug. But with the passage of time, I can now see the wisdom behind it. I now know what he meant. Beware the fickleness of fortune, for all glory is fleeting; don't be a slave to your baser desires; and most importantly, know that you may be on top today, but that all good fortune can be snatched away in an instant. Life has a way of compensating for great success by allocating us a measure of bitterness. Good fortune and ill-fortune are handmaidens, and will both appear at our doorstep. Over a long enough time span, a man's fortune always reverts to the mean.

Consider the career of the philosopher Boethius (A.D. 475?—524). In style and substance, he straddles the worlds of classical antiquity and the Christian Middle Ages in equal measure. Coming from a wealthy and distinguished Roman family, he received the best education of his day, becoming erudite in both Greek and Latin letters. Not content with scholarly pursuits, he decided to enter public life, and awed the Roman Senate with his eloquence and his benevolence to the poor. Eventually he rose to serve the Gothic king Theodoric, who ruled Italy. Boethius's abilities made him enemies, and he eventually was wrongfully accused of participation in a conspiracy against the king. Theodoric, infirm of mind and body, probably listened to the counsel of his Gothic ministers, who likely resented

Boethius's popularity among the people of Rome; and Boethius did not help his cause by proving himself inept in the game of palace intrigue.

We see a familiar theme played out here. A man of ability and substance, confident in his mastery of his environment, brought down by the malevolence of a tyrant and the spider-webs of court intrigue. A man of virtue should be as far away from a tyrant as possible. Plutarch, in his sketch of the life of Pompey, quotes a line from Sophocles on the danger of tyranny:

> He who enters a tyrant's door
> Though free before
> Shall be owned by him
> Forever more.

Trying to deal equitably with a tyrant is a mistake that has been made by many. Power not only corrupts, but it also poisons, the soul, and renders it incapable of feeling. The habit of arbitrary exercise of power becomes an addictive tonic to the tyrant, rendering him unfit for normal human interaction. One wonders why Boethius could not sense that he was out of his element in trying to deal with his employer's crafty ministers. For all his bookish wisdom, he could not see that the wisest thing of all is to keep oneself out of a dungeon. A man of virtue simply cannot mingle with those of a base nature. They will sense his virtue, in the way he speaks, in the way he dresses, and in the way he comports himself; and they will instinctively hate him as the embodiment of everything that is better than they. The good man should seek out only other good men, and avoid the rest. Men can forgive anything except virtue.

With regard to Theodoric, it is clear that his conduct on the throne displays the truth of the maxim that the habit of arbitrarily exercising power is easy to begin, but difficult to stop. Certainly Boethius's rhetorical training would have put him into contact with the historian Sallust. He might have recalled with profit this passage from the historian's great monograph *Bellum Catilinae* (The War With Catiline):

> All bad examples from the past arise from good actions. But when power goes to ignorant men or men who are not virtuous, that new precedent is transferred from those who are worthy and deserving, to those who are undeserving. The Spartans, having defeated the Athenians, imposed thirty men over them to govern them. At first, these men executed without trial those men who were the most wicked and hated. The people approved these actions and said that they were merited. But later, when their freedom of action increased, the tyrants began to execute both good men and bad at their whims, and intimidate the rest. In this way was the state reduced to slavery; it had paid a high penalty for its frivolous joy.[13]

Leaders, once given significant power, hesitate to relinquish it. For a more recent example, we have only to look at some of the events of our own time. After the terrorist attacks on the United States in September, 2001, the government asked for—and was given—sweeping powers to monitor, interdict, and detain potential terrorists. The National Security Agency (NSA) was given essentially *carte blanche* to conduct intrusive monitoring of nearly anyone it desired to monitor, all in the name of national security. The Congress and the public gave little thought to the consequences of these new powers; all dissenting voices were drowned out beneath a chorus of patriotism and martial enthusiasm. It later became clear that these powers were being

---

[13] *Bellum Catilinae*, 51.32.

exercised arbitrarily, and that what was intended as a temporary security measure had become a regular practice. But this is how power behaves. Once gained, it is not relinquished. Leaders exercising such powers are riding a tiger, and know that if they dare get off, the raging animal may consume them.

Theodoric eventually had Boethius thrown in jail and sentenced to death. It was a shocking reversal for a man who had during his entire life known nothing but success. And from this miserable place, he wrote one of the first books of prison literature, and perhaps the most famous of all medieval books: *De consolatione philosophae* (The Consolation of Philosophy). Nothing focuses the mind as wonderfully as a death sentence. Drawing strength and solace from his classical studies, he set out timeless principles of fortune, fate, and how to seek the good life. In all his book, there is not one word of complaining. Fortune is various and fickle, says Boethius, and a wise man benefits more from bad luck than from good:

> For I suppose that adverse fortune does more good for men than good fortune. Fortune always, when seen to be flattering with the face of felicity, lies; but she is always truthful when she shows her instability by changing. That type of fortune lies, but this one instructs us. That type ties the minds of those who enjoy good things with a deceitful appearance. The other releases us with the awareness of the fragility of happiness. Thus you may see that one [type of fortune] is as fickle as the wind, flowing on her own accord and ultimately unknown, and the other [type of fortune] is sober, fully-equipped, and prudent with the experience of adversity.[14]

---

[14] *De Consol. Philos.* II.8

The rich man, in his stupidity and venality, will hoard wealth, not realizing that it will all eventually be taken away:

And may he bear around his neck pearls of the Red Sea, and plough his fertile land with a hundred oxen! Biting concern will never leave him as he stands, and his light wealth will not follow him in death.[15]

Boethius suggests that a wise man, if he enjoys great success, will always remember to behave in a modest and virtuous way. Why? Because the people he encountered on his rise to the top will be the same ones who will witness his fall. Never mock or insult those worse off than you; one day, you will be among them. A wise man will not count it an evil if he encounters adversity, for this will test and harden him:

A wise man ought not to get upset, every time he is brought into a contest with fortune, just as it would not be fitting for a brave man to be indignant when faced with the crashing sound of war. Since for each of these the difficulty is of the same substance: for propagating glory, and for fashioning wisdom. And this is indeed why virtue is called virtue, because striving with its own strength, it is not overcome by adversity….You join mental battle fiercely with every kind of fortune, lest depression oppress you or prosperity corrupt you.[16]

And finally, we cannot call someone a real man who is driven and controlled by lusts. Chasing after sensual or material

---

[15] *D.C.P.*, III.3.
[16] *D.C.P.*, IV.7.45

pleasures is demeaning, debasing, and brutalizing. Employing a string of animal analogies, he says:

> He who burns with avarice, the violent stealer of others' wealth? You would call him a wolf. The ferocious and unstable man who exercises his tongue in litigation? You would compare him to a dog. The scammer rejoices to have plundered by frauds? He is on the level of a little fox...The weak and fearful who fears what should not be feared? He is like a deer. The stupid fool is inert? He lives like a donkey...He is submerged in foul and nasty desires? He is detained by his own sordid desires.[17]

The overall impression given by the *Consolation* is that, on a long enough timeline, a man's fortune will revert to the mean. Even if he is garlanded by success, this will eventually be counterbalanced by the visitation of some calamity. The universe, which he equates with God, has some built-in balancing principle, so that our successes will sooner or later be offset with misfortunes. With this in mind, the wise man will behave accordingly. Cherish your true friends, for you will know who they are when disaster hits you. Do not denigrate those less fortunate than you, for you may find yourself among them. Do not tempt Fate by allowing yourself to be enslaved with pursuits for women, money, and glory. All of these things will be taken away from you in time.

The profundity of Boethius's philosophy is matched by the poignant tragedy of his fate. On October 23, 524, the Reaper finally called on him. His executioners removed him from his cell,

---

[17] D.C.P., IV.3.60.

looped a cord around his neck, and strangled him. The injustice of this end is overshadowed by the brilliance of his philosophical testament to the world. May we, in our hour of crisis, face our challenges with equal courage and stoic resolution. And if we think we know better than the world, and if we think we are exempt from the laws of fortune, we should think again. Time, work, and the vagaries of fate will chasten our pretentions to rebelliousness. The world will teach us, whether we want the lesson or not.

6. I Am The Isthmus

It is a shame that many of the best short stories of H.G. Wells have been forgotten. They showcase his keen interest in science and technology, along with a burning sense of moral rectitude. It is not what one would expect from an author of "scientific romances" (as he would say). Compare Conan Doyle's science fiction short stories with those of Wells. Doyle was a prankster, a trickster, with a bent for sadistic turns of plot and characterization. When I first heard that Doyle was suspected for being responsible for the Piltdown Man hoax that fooled many of the best and brightest, I was not surprised. He certainly was capable of pulling off a stunt like that.

But Wells was a bit different. He's not concerned with sadistic turns of plot. He wants to make utopias. And this is what we have to keep telling ourselves as we read anything by him: Wells is a moralist, first and foremost. He is concerned with the creation of earthly utopias. Or, failing in creating them, pointing out the way to construct them. Wells is a moral edifice-builder: the greatest moralist of all the Victorian writers.

But if only we could live up to his ideals. Morality! Goodness! How I long to be good, to be moral. Or, more likely, how I long *to be seen* to be good and moral. I remember a quote I heard once—and I can't recall from whom—that went something like this: "I don't know what is in the hearts of evil men. But I know what is in the heart of a good man, and it is horrible."

Because we can't live up to the standards Herbert George wants to set for us, you see. Wells wants so desperately for man to be good, noble, and socialist, and concerned about his fellow man. Poor Herbert! He had the bad luck to live through not just one, but two, world wars, and found out to his chagrin that his beloved science was at last neutral in the great game of life. All his hopes and dreams came crashing down about him, one after the other. He died in 1945, convinced that man had proven himself incapable of long-term survival as a species. One of his last books was called *The World Set Free*. And poor Herbert himself was set free by death soon after. Herbert was never able to accept the idea that science is neutral. Neutral, meaning able to both help and hurt man. An indifferent force, a factor among many in a turbulent Cosmos with its atoms swerving about in their Lucretian inclinations and declinations, and where flux is the only constant. As Lucretius says:

> For the Ages transform the nature of the world, and one
> state of things ought to move into
> Another, and not one thing remains similar as before.
> All things move about, all nature transitions, and
> compels change.[18]

But Herbert's problems are mostly self-inflicted. For he won't just let man be man. He can't just leave biology alone. He always insists on trying to make man—this "trousered ape" as Will Durant calls us humans—some sort of latent Ideal Man. And if we only try hard enough, if only we can master enough science and technology, we can become this Ideal Man. Wells believes that

---

[18]Mutat enim mundi naturam totius aetas,
ex alioque alius status excipere omnia debet,
nec manet ulla sui similis res: omnia migrant,
omnia commutat natura et vertere cogit. (*De Rerum Natura* V.826)

$$\text{Man + technology = Utopia.}$$

Whereas the real equation is;

$$\text{Man + technology} = 0$$

Meaning that man and technology combine to form: nothing. Nothing, basically. Man plus technology equals man with more technology. We change our means, but not our purposes. Technology can help us travel faster, reshape the earth, and do a thousand other things. But in the end, it provides us no moral advancement. It is neutral. Everything cancels out to nothing. And there you have it. All our technological development of the past hundred years has brought us no corresponding advance in moral development. Until we can change our goals and purposes, science will forever be a new means of achieving an old end. But this was too dark a truth for poor Herbert. He couldn't bring himself to accept this. It was man himself who was the problem, he believed. And so he raged against the world, stumbled from one Utopian dream to another in Russia or England, and finally gave up the game altogether. Why, oh why, couldn't he accept it?

Because he couldn't. He just could not.

But he knew. Deep inside, in his heart of hearts, he knew the primal nature of man, his reptilian, slithery essence. And this is what makes H.G. a great and tragic figure: his brave clinging to an ideal that he knew was doomed.

Doomed.

Because it is of no use to chase futilely after the material things of this world. In the end, they leave us only craving for more and more, a feedback loop of ever-increasing avarice. It is trite, and it is an old idea. But it is true. The worthy goal of every man's "game" should only be the improvement of his Self, the polishing of his own soul. It is this soul which will function as the Isthmus between the world of corporeal form and the world of imagination: that fine dividing entity—which the mystic Ibn Arabi called the *barzakh* (برزخ)— thinly separating the world of the real with the world of the unreal. It divides both, but contains elements of both within it. Only this smoothly polished Isthmus can effectively mediate between the world of imagination and the world of the real. All else is idle vanity. I call these lines below *I Am The Isthmus*:

I.

The world is a palestra of anxieties,
A spectacle of wrongs and iniquities,
And a vale of tears watering the rising
Orchids of our discontent.
It is a threshing floor of temptations for the unwary,
And a churning sea, turbid with the color
Of false hopes and virtues so inadequate
In duration and amplitude.
You have read my words here many times,
But you have not truly heard me,
Preferring the savory illusions of your idle expectations,
And the flitting, dissolving mayas of your own transitory phantoms,
Which fade, softly, into the swirling mist of memory,
Leaving you ever hungrier, O my brother, for
A food to nourish your soul, and detumesce the
Angry, swollen, and searching heart.
When will you believe what your eyes tell you,
And what your senses command you!
You know the problem, and you sense the solution.
Yet you lack the conviction to speak it, and to practice it.
Solace cannot be found in the endless chase of the material,
For this world, this mirror of vanities, withholds its

Pleasure as easily as it grants it, leaving you empty and
Seeking more and more, a ceaseless quest of the
insatiate.
When will you hear me, you bondsman to your lusts,
You blind man on your blind journey?
You read me, but you do not feel me.
You endorse me, but you hear me not.

II.

The only game that there is, and that will ever be,
Is the game of You, and only You.
All else is illusion, a cruel joke, a heartless deceiver.
All solutions reside within you, and are there for your
Drawing, as raw sap is tapped from Vermont maple.
Nothing exists but you, you, as the Isthmus
Between the word of the corporeal, and
The world of the spiritual, the world of imagination.
The Isthmus divides and joins these two worlds,
As two seas that meet together, never fully merging.
It is you, this Isthmus, that separates the known
From the unknown, the existent from the nonexistent,
The negated from the affirmed, the understandable
From the incomprehensible.
You are the Isthmus, the joiner of the Two Worlds,
And retaining elements of both.
Why do you not seek your true purpose?
Why do you not take your seat on this throne?
The only game there is, is the spiritual game of You, the
game
Which improves your Soul, and
Fortifies you from this world's ceaseless pantomime of
injustice.
This polished and prepared Soul will then truly be the
lordly

Isthmus, the arbiter of worlds, the mediator of its own
fate.
And when you know this, and truly mediate between the
Two Worlds,
As you were intended to,
You will become the master of all that is,
And all that will ever be.

Wells knew his ideals were doomed, and yet he persisted.
One is reminded of Pascal's famous line about man and the
Cosmos. Despite man's insignificance before eternity, says
Pascal, and his certain destruction by cosmic forces, man is still
nobler than the Cosmos who may destroy him. For of its victory
over man, the indifferent Cosmos knows nothing, while man
knows he is dying.

His 1905 story *Aepyornis Island* highlights this inner conflict.
The plot: a biologist exploring remote regions in Madagascar
hunts for evidence of an immense, long-extinct flightless bird
called *Aepyornis vastissimus*. Never seen by European eyes, the
bird stood nearly fifteen feet tall and supposedly died out in the
1400s. The biologist narrator chances upon a nest of melon-sized
eggs in a jungle swamp, preserved for centuries by some freak of
climate and soil, and takes them away in his boat. The boat
becomes wrecked soon after, and the biologist finds himself
marooned on a deserted island with a *Aepyornis* egg. The egg
hatches, and out comes this feathered anachronism after hundreds
of years of hibernation. It is very cute, at first. The biologist
showers it with love, attention, and care. All seems blissfully
wonderful. Idyllic. On a deserted island. And our biologist is
enraptured.

And then things turn very sour.

As the *Aepyornis* bird reaches adulthood, the biologist comes
uncomfortably aware that it is not a precious snowflake. It has a
nasty and foul temper. It is greedy. And cruel. Soon enough the

colossal bird attacks him, delivering sledge-hammer kicks, and then it is all-out warfare. The once loving couple now stalk each other over the island, with savage bloodlust, in a vicious fight to the death. In the last scene, the biologist grapples furiously with the bird by the shoreline, sawing at its neck with his rusty knife in a murderous rage, hot blood spilling over the pure white sand. We recall the desperate death-battle in Jack London's *Love of Life*, where a starving man and wolf stalk each other across a frozen wasteland in a horrifying fight to the death. What are we to make of such a story? Is it just another variation on the "be careful what you wish for" cliché?

Consider the bird. Is he a symbol? *Of course*. But of what, exactly?

He is a symbol of our innermost, deepest Holy Grail. Our deepest Blood-Desire. Every man's sacred quest is etched into his bones from the moment he is born. He cannot escape this destiny. He can dodge his quest for some time, but in the end, if he wishes to become truly fulfilled, he must take up the quest. And man, like the biologist in the story, is required to chase down and possess this hidden, Sacred Chalice. Required to: if we are to be men. We nurture this wish, covet it, and care for it, as the biologist did with his precious and ancient cargo of eggs.

And then: chase it down, this Holy Grail, show it no mercy. Kill it, in order to possess it utterly. And this is ever a pretty sight. For the process of hunting down and possessing our deepest desire is never clean and easy; because part of you dies in the process. It can be a ghastly, brutal process. Blood is going to run into the white sand, and form obscene clumps about our feet. And yet this is necessary, a sacred requirement of our Great Transition. For it is only in this way that man can advance, grow, and move forward. The hunting down and destruction of our own inner Holy Grail is exactly like being reborn. Man and his tools—even if he has only a rusty knife—are enough for him to master his environment. We don't negate each other, we complement each other. I am a man, and I am master of my environment. I am a man!

And in the right hands, my dull, rusty knife here by my side is enough. We need only the will to use it. Because there is no other way, really. If we are to move forward to our own Great Day as men, we must go through this mortal hunt. This chasing down of our innermost Blood-Being and Blood-Desire. Even if it means we must grapple with our own inner, prehistoric monsters, and fight them to the death with blood bubbling into our clean white sand, it must still be done.

And there is no going back: for this reversion would be the death of us, as men. It would be a real spiritual abandonment, and a corresponding degeneration of us as men. We just can't go back. The biologist couldn't go back, you can't go back, and I know that I could never go back, either. So it is only forward, forward, forward.

And once we accept this, it will be the dawn of our own Great Day: A Great Day that is transformative and redemptive, in accordance with the rules of that mystic quest that was etched into our bones from the moment of our creation.

7. A Program Of Education

There is a perception that "education" involves stuffing one's head with facts and information. What passes for male education these days is often a travesty, for it places far too much emphasis on intellectual development, and attaches too little importance to the training of character. Boys have been looked upon as defective girls, needing constant suppression of their healthy instincts to make them more feminine. The consequences of this policy have been disastrous for the transmission of masculine virtues to the next generation. The cultivation of leadership qualities in men is a critical component of character building, and yet the idea that it should actually be taught has nearly vanished from organized education. Political correctness and various feminist pet doctrines have taken the place of training in the masculine ethic; even the military, long the last bastion of masculine virtue, is well on its way to becoming a feminized social welfare organization. One could argue that what men of today lack the most is vigorous training in character and leadership. The historian Sallust, in his *War With Catiline*, puts into the mouth of Caesar a masterful speech that contains a few choice words on what virtues made the Romans great:

> Do not believe our ancestors to have made our country great from a small size by force of arms. If this was so, we would by far have a more beautiful nation, since we have a larger quantity of citizens and allies than they, as well as armaments and horses. But there were other qualities that made them great, of which we have none:

industriousness in the household, a just rule, in deliberation a free spirit gripped by neither bad conduct nor passion. Instead, we have opulence and greed, public poverty and private extravagance. We praise riches, but pursue slothfulness. No discrimination is made between good men and bad, and ambition possesses all the rewards of virtue. And it is no wonder. When each of you takes advice separately for his own self-interest, when you are servants to physical pleasure (*voluptas*) at home, and here to money and influence (*gratia*), it follows from this that it constitutes an attack on the republic.[19]

This could almost be a summary of the American scene today. Many of the modern man's problems—apathy and waywardness, lack of confidence, catty behavior towards other men, lack of focus and intensity, and weakness of mind or body— can be attributed to the gross deficiencies of our educational system, as well as to the complete lack of mentorship for young men. A remedy for this malaise can easily be found if only we have the courage to re-examine the practices of our ancestors. Consider, for example, the educational views of Italian humanist Pier Paolo Vergerio as expressed in his treatise *De ingenuis moribus et liberalibus adulescentiae studiis liber* (*Book on the Character and Studies Befitting a Free-Born Youth*).

Born in 1370 in Capodistria (what is today Koper, in Slovenia), Vergerio taught rhetoric and law in Padua, Florence, and Bologna, and served for a time as an advisor to the Holy Roman Emperor Sigismund. His educational essay for men, composed around 1402, is a near-perfect summary of the

---

[19] *Bellum Catilinae* 52.20.

Renaissance idea of education for young leaders. It was republished numerous times in the following centuries, and had considerable influence. It is a pity (though not surprising) that it is not more widely known today. For nearly alone among his contemporaries, Vergerio was a firm proponent of the idea that everyone has different talents, and that an educational program must be adapted to each student's strengths and weaknesses. Vergerio's main points are summarized below. I then offer my own conclusions and commentary.

1. Education in character begins in the cradle. Parents should pick a name for a boy that is not "unseemly" or clownish. The correct choice of name is a matter of high importance, despite the cavalier manner with which most women treat it. Names can affect character, and nothing is worse than being saddled with an oafish or irritating name. While this point may at first glance seem to be a minor one, further thought suggests otherwise. The development of masculine virtue requires an environment conducive to its growth and nourishment. And environment begins with nominative identity.

2. Parents should settle their sons in "renowned cities" (*in egregibus urbibus*). Few opportunities will be found in the middle of nowhere, and men need the company of other good men to develop themselves.

3. Although training in the liberal arts should start at an early age, parents should take care to direct sons to those studies for which they are naturally inclined. Compulsion in education is something that should be used in careful moderation.

4. Body and mind are connected intimately. Just as a healthy body consumes and digests food well, so a healthy mind will not scorn anyone, but will put the best interpretation on what it hears or learns.

5. Young men should look at themselves in the mirror often. There is nothing wrong with this, and it serves a useful function. Those with a fine appearance will not dishonor themselves with

vices, and those with an average or ugly appearance will strive to make themselves more attractive with their virtues.

6. Young men are generous and open-minded by nature because they have rarely experienced want and need. They are also credulous, due to their lack of worldly experience. Their opinions can change easily and quickly. They take great pleasure in their friendships and love the clubs they belong to, which they often "join and abandon on the same day." Leadership instruction must be given while taking into account these qualities.

7. Every age of a man's life has vices particular to it: adolescence "burns with lust", middle age is "rocked with ambition", and old age "wastes away in greed." Not everyone is this way, but men are more inclined to these vices according to their age.

8. Young men must be taught from an early age to treat the elderly with "profound reverence." Much can be learned from a young man's associating with an older man. So Roman youth treated senators and other older men with deference, thereby learning much about perseverance and patience.

9. Young men should learn right away the value of being constructively criticized and admonished. This is necessary for personal improvement. People who don't listen to anything they dislike are "the ones most vulnerable to deception." The weak stomach is the one that "will only accept delicacies."

10. Excessive leniency can corrupt a young man. Women are unsuited to the task of training a man for male leadership. Those who have been "brought up in luxury under widowed mothers" display these negative traits most openly. However, this problem is easily corrected provided the proper male role models appear, one way or another.

11. The finest studies for leadership are those based on arms (military) and letters (history, philosophy, languages, and rhetoric). Everyone wants to be learned in old age, but to achieve this one must start early and exert "zealous effort." Being learned

in letters and arms will provide a remedy against "sloth" and solace in the face of worry and stress.

12. The ancient Greeks trained young leaders by teaching letters, wrestling, music, and drawing. This sort of regimen gave them appreciation for the "beauty and charm of things both natural and artificial." Vergerio goes even further. "Great men", he says, "need to be able to talk among themselves and make judgments about matters of this kind."

13. Good disciplines to know also are literature, in that it forms good habits of virtue, and strengthens the memory by study. Rhetoric (the art of eloquence) and disputation are required also for being able to verbally spar with opponents in the inevitable contests that will confront any leader. Poetics is good for relaxation, mathematics and the sciences good for logical development, and languages for getting outside oneself.

14. Don't just dip into any authors. Surround yourself only with the very best. By keeping company with great men, we will learn greatness by association. The most important quality in education is hunger: that fanatical desire to learn and better oneself. Some students have it, some do not. An astute teacher will be alert to the right signs from a pupil, and know how to cultivate the passion for learning and achievement.

15. The easiest person to deceive is our own self, and self-deception only damages the deceiver. Young men must confer often with peers and guides, so as not to form an inflated opinion of themselves.

16. The training of the body is of paramount importance. It should be conditioned from a young age for rigorous service, military ability, and endurance. Young men should be hardened from a young age to endure pain and discomfort of all sorts, so that they are not broken by the strains of life and struggle. They should also be taught to "dare great things." The Cretans and Spartans valued hunting, running, wrestling, and jumping, and

sought ways to train themselves to endure hunger, thirst, cold, and heat. Luxuries weaken the mind and body.

17. In a great quote, Vergerio reminds us that "Every period of life has the capacity to yield something splendid."[20]

18. The youth should set fixed hours for bodily exercise every day, and fixed hours for the exercise of the mind. Strict self-discipline is critical. The emperor Theodosius, he notes, would engage in military exercises or legal judgments by day, and in the evenings would apply himself to his studies by lamplight.

19. Since battle tactics are constantly changing, a forward thinking youth will attempt to master the martial arts and self-defense arts of his day. This should include mastery of weaponry, personal combat skills, horsemanship, and movement over rugged terrain carrying heavy loads or equipment. There are many different kinds of combat. "For things are done one way in a melee; another when the decision rests on a battle formation; another when there is an infantry charge, and another when combat takes the form of a duel."

20. Expect often to be unfairly judged. Generals get the praise for the valor of their soldiers, but also get scorn for their shortcomings. "The glory that comes from good deeds is unequal to the shame that comes from mistakes."

21. Learn to swim well. It greatly increases confidence.

22. Rest and leisure is of vital importance. Hunting, team sports, and fishing "refresh the spirit with great delight, and the movement they require fortifies the limbs."

23. Dancing and cavorting with women is also essential, and there is a "certain profit in doing them, since they exercise the

---

[20] Habet namque omnis aetas, ut edere magnificum aliquid possit. (Vergerio, 59). Latin text from Kallendorf, C.W. (ed.) *Humanist Educational Treatises*, Cambridge: Harvard Univ. Press, 2002.

body and bring dexterity to the limbs, if they do not make young men lustful and vain, corrupting good behavior."

24. From time to time, however, "one needs to do absolutely nothing and be entirely free from work, so as to meet once again the demands of work and toil. For the muscle which is always stretched taut usually breaks if it is not sometimes relaxed."

25. Grooming the body is critically important. The end result should be neither "too fastidious nor too slovenly." Excessive focus on grooming is "a sign of a feminine mind and a proof of great vanity."

26. Do not associate with clowns or fools. Bad conversation can corrupt good character.[21]

27. The passion for learning can become an impediment if pursued too relentlessly. This can happen if a student desires to take on more information than he can handle; he flits about from one subject to another, achieving little mastery of what is important. A large quantity of information "ingested at once" has the same effect as a large amount of food consumed too quickly: the body is weighed down and rendered inert. It is better to devote oneself to one thing and pursue it to a successful level of achievement, than to embrace and reject one thing after another. "Wines turn sour", he says with a with a twinkle in his eye, "when they are rebottled too often."[22]

All in all, this advice is an excellent program for training in leadership and character. For a short treatise, Vergerio's points can scarcely be improved on. It is a stern ethic, owing much to his classical predecessors in overall tone and content. It is a bit heavy on arms and letters, but we must remember that Vergerio was

------

[21] Corrumpunt bonos mores colloquia mala. (Vergerio, 13, quoting St. Jerome's *Epistulae 70*)

[22] Acescunt vina quae saepius transvasantur. (Vergerio, 51).

writing before the sciences became part of the Western curricula; and he was more concerned with character development than with quantitative knowledge. His counsel was directed at individuals, but we should note that masculine virtue does not exist in isolation. It thrives only when certain conditions are met. In my own view, the following conditions must exist as a precondition to the flowering of the masculine ethic: (1) institutional support from some sector of society, such as the military, an organized religion, or mercantile and business guilds; (2) the existence of fraternal societies, where men can congregate and associate separately from women, without fear of running afoul of politically correct restrictions and constraints; and (3) mentors willing to instruct young men.

Unfortunately, none of the conditions needed for the cultivation of masculine virtue are present in modern America. Institutions that once nurtured it have been marginalized or destroyed, and mentorship is now a purely hit-or-miss affair. The way forward has been laid out before us; it only remains to be seen whether we have the conviction to follow it.

8. THE WISDOM OF ARISTIPPUS

The student of philosophy navigates perilous waters. Some of the great writers in the field, ancient and modern, were depressing or abnormal men, who consoled themselves in their solitude by spinning spider-webs of metaphysics or elaborate edifices of rhetoric. Others conducted forays into opaque logic-chopping; and still others take refuge in sanctimonious moralizing. In all this confusion, it is refreshing finally to find a philosopher who is wise enough to try to be happy.

Aristippus of Cyrene (c. 435-356 B.C.) was a pupil of Socrates who found it expedient to leave Athens after the execution of his teacher. He apparently incurred the wrath of his fellow students Plato and Xenophon for not participating in Socrates's bedside vigil before his death. Well-built, handsome, and socially adept, he became popular in the city of Cyrene (located on the coast of North Africa) and eventually founded his own influential school of philosophy there.

His philosophy was frankly sensualist and material. All that we do, he claimed, is structured around seeking pleasure and avoiding pain; thus, pleasure is the ultimate good, and the goal of philosophy should be to find ways of experiencing pleasure within healthy and meaningful boundaries. The wise man should put a greater emphasis on physical and material pleasures than on intellectual or moral ones, since tomorrow is uncertain, and we can only be assured of the present. He who has mastered the art of enjoying pleasures without endangering his health or safety can best be called wise, not the self-denying ascetic crouching in a cave and fleeing from the responsibilities of life. Enjoyment of pleasures should never extend so far that one becomes enslaved by their pursuit: "I possess", he famously said, "but I am not possessed."

Although he eventually became wealthy and moved among the aristocratic classes, he had known poverty in his life, and was famous for having borne both conditions with dignity and grace.

Demonstrating that lucre was not incompatible with the dignity of philosophical speculation, he was the first of Socrates's pupils to charge fees for giving instruction to others. He cared little for the opinions of others, frequently laughed at authority and laws, and openly co-habited with a beautiful and well-known courtesan named Lais. The true wise man was not the narrow-minded bookworm, but that man who had known a variety of sensual pleasures and was able to assert his mastery over them. Diogenes Laertius, in his *Lives of the Philosophers*, tells many anecdotes about his wit and wisdom, of which the following extracts are my favorites ("he" here below refers to Aristippus):

When he was spat on by King Dionysius I of Syracuse (in whose court he worked), someone asked him how he could endure such abuse. He replied, "If fishermen let themselves be drenched with seawater in pursuit of fish, should not I also endure a wetting to spread wisdom?"

Diogenes (a rival) was once washing dirt from his vegetables, saw Aristippus walking by, and scoffed at him, saying, "If you had learned how to make these part of your diet, you would not have paid court to kings." To which he replied, "And if you knew how to associate with men, you would not be washing vegetables."

When he was once asked what he gained from philosophy, he said, "The ability to feel at ease in any society."

When he was once asked what advantage philosophers have, he replied, "Should all laws be repealed, we will go on living as we do now."

When King Dionysius once asked him why philosophers go to rich men's homes, while rich men do not visit philosophers, he replied that "the one know what they need, while the other do not."

When he was asked how the educated differ from the uneducated, he replied, "Exactly as horses that have been trained differ from untrained horses."

When he once visited the house of a courtesan with one of his students, the pupil became embarrassed. Aristippus said, "It is not going in that is dangerous, but being unable to go out."

When someone remarked that philosophers were always seen at rich men's homes, he said, "So, too, doctors attend to those who are sick, but no one for that reason would prefer being sick to being a doctor."

He once said that he did not take money from his friends for his own use, but to teach them upon what objects their money should be spent.

Being asked what was the difference between the wise man and the unwise man, he said, "Dress them both in the plainest, simplest clothing, and send them among strangers. Watch them, and you will know."

To one man who boasted that he could drink a great deal without getting drunk, Aristippus replied, "And so can a mule."

To those who criticized him for keeping house with the courtesan Lais, he replied, "I have Lais, not she me; and it is not abstinence from pleasures that is best, but mastery over them without ever being ruined."

When a courtesan once told him that she was bearing his child, he replied, "You are no more sure of this than if, after running through a thicket of thorn bushes, you were to say that you knew which branch had pricked you."

Someone once criticized him for taking money from King Dionysius at the same time that Plato had published an excellent book. "Well", he said, "I want money, and Plato wants books."[23]

In our final judgment, there is much good to be found in Aristippus's philosophy. Like many of the philosophical schools of antiquity, it had the shortcomings of a belief system that made no appeal to the supernatural for solace and consolation. And are we really certain that people exclusively structure their lives around the pursuit of pleasure and avoidance of pain? Does not such a sensual view of the world invite all sorts of abuses by immature or undeveloped minds? Can such a philosophy provide

---

[23] See Diog. Laert. II.65-66. (translation by R.D. Hicks, from *Diogenes Laertius: Lives of the Eminent Philosophers,* Cambridge: Harvard Univ. Press, 2006).

consolation to us in our grief, tribulations, and struggles? Men need myths, gods, and rituals to inspire him; Aristippus was able only to offer a purely moral code. In this respect, his vision suffered from the same defects as Stoicism and Epicureanism: for a moral message really to take root, some fire and brimstone must be behind the gentle admonitions. Nevertheless, his influence was considerable. His school continued on after his death, and was gradually subsumed into the surging tide of Epicureanism which was to arrive after his death.

In response to his critics, Aristippus would argue that he never advocated for unrestrained hedonism, but only for the balanced enjoyment of select pleasures. The goal of life was to juggle enjoyment while avoiding personal catastrophe. Like any good pitch-man or promoter, some of his statements seem to have been deliberately intended to rile up his opponents. Despite obvious faults, his teaching was an honest attempt to bring philosophy down from the rarefied Platonic clouds and back to the hurly-burly of real life. And if practicing what one preaches is the final measure of a man, Aristippus must be counted among the most sincere philosophers of antiquity. He was beloved by many, and hated by none. According to one historian, he believed the most inspiring sight in the world was the spectacle of a virtuous man pursuing his goals in the midst of vile people. Who among us can find fault with this verdict?

9. REVOLT AGAINST THE EXCESS OF REVOLT

I have recently been reading the autobiography of one of my favorite historians, Will Durant. The book is entitled *Dual Autobiography*, as it outlines the life not just of Will Durant, but also the life of his wife Ariel. Mrs. Durant assisted her husband so considerably in the later stages of his monumental opus *The Story of Civilization* that she was given the credit of co-authorship of the final volumes. Their life struggles and trials make for fascinating reading. I had always admired them for their literary accomplishments, and was happy to discover that I could admire them for their personal qualities as well.

One passage caught my eye. Mrs. Durant describes a lecture she delivered in 1927 to a group of "modern women" (what would now be called feminists). The topic of the lecture was the ultimate purpose of female "emancipation." Daring to take an unpopular line with her ardent assemblage of auditors, she urged women not to cast off their traditional roles too hastily. Her words are so prescient, and so uncannily accurate, that I should quote them here at length:

> I accepted the emancipation of woman as a natural result of the continuing Industrial Revolution, replacing domestic drudgery with gadgets and cans…But if emancipation meant a revolt against marriage, and an exaltation of career above motherhood, it would bring a regrettable masculinity in women and a corresponding effeminacy in men. What will be the gain when women wear pants and men have soprano voices?…What shall

we say of the many abnormalities that have increased in...our age of transition? The progress of inversion, perversion... a third sex? ... Have we the right to say anything if men wistfully long for a home while women crowd tearooms, cafes, and cabarets? ... So I pleaded for moderation, for "a revolt against the excess of revolt."[24]

Remember that these words were delivered in 1927. They predict precisely that trajectory of gender relations that has played out in the past eighty years; and unfortunately, we are forced to admit that Mrs. Durant's admonitions were prophecy. We now have precisely the type of society she warned us to avoid: female exaltation of career over all else, the masculinization of women, the corresponding effeminacy of men, and the rise of an androgynous, freakish, and neutered "third sex" that has completely withdrawn from the human mating game. These are the general contours of American society in 2014.

Inevitably, another question arises. Are these changes part of the natural, inevitable process of human evolution, or are they simply symptoms of our civilization's decay? The question is a critical one. For if these changes are a natural outgrowth of technological development, then we are forced to admit that traditional masculinity is doomed. The human male may himself become an evolutionary dead end, fit to join that long list of other extinct genera of humans: *paranthropus bosiei, homo austraopithecus, homo neanderthalensis*, etc. Take your pick. It is not out of the question. My imagination was fired a few years ago when I read of the discovery in 2003 of *homo floresiensis* in Indonesia. What an incredible story! Anthropologists poking

---

[24] Durant, W. & A., *Dual Autobiography*, New York: Simon and Schuster, 1977, p. 121.

about in caves in the remote islands of the Indonesian archipelago find bones that first are mistaken for humans with stunted development. It is now generally accepted that this diminutive "hobbit man" constituted a distinct species of human, and may have been alive as late as 14,000 years ago. Imagine that: an entirely different species of humanoid, coexisting with modern man on remote islands in Indonesia. I wonder what H.G. Wells would have made of all this.

Even more recently, news reports announced the discovery in China of another new species of Stone Age human, called "Red Deer People." This type apparently also existed as recently as 11,000 to 14,000 years ago. In evolutionary terms, 14,000 years is the blink of an eye. What a strange, wondrous world this is! The point here is that social changes, in the long run, can have serious consequences for the survival of the species. Like any organism, the human type is constantly branching and sub-branching out in endless evolutionary gropings, with Darwinian certitude; some of these variations will prove to be useful, and add survival value to the race. Some will add no value, and become dead ends; or they will become superseded by other types in Nature's infinite capacity for variation. The deliberate destruction of the masculine ethic in the West may, over time, set modern man down the path of extinction: those bloated, wretched freaks lurching about in the aisles of the average suburban Walmart store may be a frightening portent of humanity's future.

But I cannot bring myself to believe this. This would be a future too dark to contemplate. I prefer to believe that our current social woes are a temporary hiccup in the later stages of that Industrial Revolution which has haunted mankind since the 1780s. No doubt old James Watt, tinkering with his steam engines in England at that time, could never have foreseen the social consequences of his revolution. Yet we should curse him just the same.

Call me delusional. But I prefer to take the position that feminist excesses and abuses will eventually prompt a furious backlash from both men and women. Mrs. Durant's exhortation for a "revolt against the excess of revolt" will become a reality, as the oligarchs running Western societies realize that they cannot sit atop a social dung heap and govern effectively. A corrective movement will be born (or may already be here) that will seek to restore a natural and healthy balance among the unhappy genders. If both men and women have degenerated and lost their previous vigor, perhaps this is due in America to the unparalleled period of ease and luxury of the decades since the 1930s. As Tacitus says,

> Nam militares artes per otium ignotae, industriosque aut ignavos pax in aequo tenet.[25]

In this world of tumult, this cyclone of conflict, we can only tend to the sacred flames in our inner temples, and take care that their flickering lights do not go out. For my part, I refuse to become what the prevailing social conditions want me to become. I refuse to accept *homo Walmartensis* as the prototype of man's future. I refuse to let the light die out. And if that means we go the way of the Neanderthal, or some other evolutionary dead end, then so be it. We will still be nobler and greater than the forces that destroy us, for, as Pascal says, we will know we are dying; whereas of its victory, a heedless and unfeeling society will know nothing.

---

[25] The arts of war are lost in a world of leisure, and peace levels equally both the man of action and the dullard. *Annals,* XII.12

10. THE CHANT OF THE MYSTIC

I.

Know, O my brother, that He, the One, is wholly nondelimited, and

Any attribution of attributes to Him would only impose our own

Woeful qualifiers, our own puny limitations, on his unknowable quiddity.

He is free, free of our analytic constriction and confinement, our mental

Boxes which we open and close for our categorical comfort.

Who are we to add to, or subtract from, that fecundity which is

His domain? He who created us in His own image needs no qualifiers,

No explanations, no explanatory mental gymnastics, in order to continue His

Outpouring of creative energy and all-embracing multiplicity.

I believe in every belief, I accept the tenets of every creed.

I am the prince of tasters, the sultan of samplers, the affirmer of the

Firmament, and yet still I cannot express the unity, presence,

And *wujud* of this omnipresent Master of All Things.

The latent potential of the Divine form is limitless, with every man
Manifesting such potential into existence in his own unique way.

II.

We know the One, we know Him, through his self-disclosure to us.
He manifests himself in every blade of grass, every atom in existence,
Every creature that walks, slithers, flies, swims, or swings from the
Vines of the steaming jungles of the equatorial regions.
The glass displays the qualities of its contents.
A mystic said, "Water takes on the shape of its holding glass", and this
Shows that we accept the One's self-disclosure to ourselves,
And not that we believe in the One.
We believe in this manifested self-disclosure, and not
In the unknowable source from which it emanates.
And so the One's self-disclosure to us, is ultimately us.
We worship Him not as He is, but as we perceive Him in us.
Truly, we know nothing of Him except that which He manifests
Within us. And just as the glass displays the effects of what it contains,
So the mystic perceives the unending manifestation of His
Self-disclosure in every object, in every creature, and in every thing.
The mystic knows that He discloses Himself, and

Knows why He discloses himself, but he can never ultimately
Know how He discloses Himself, for that is beyond our poor ken.

11. THE REALITY OF PROGRESS

The Roman writer Aulus Gellius relates an amusing story in his book *Attic Nights* (*Noctes Atticae,* IX.4). Returning from Greece to Italy and stopping at the port of Brundisium, he decided to visit the local market and see what was available for sale. Finding some bundles of old books by eminent Greek authors, and attracted by "their extraordinary and unexpected cheapness," he purchased them with high hopes. His enthusiasm was short-lived. After examining them on two successive nights, he found them to be filled with childish fables, incredibilities, and myths masquerading as fact. The authors assured readers, for example, that the Scythians consumed human flesh; that cyclopses existed in northern Europe; and that a race of men could be found whose feet were turned backward. Gellius was further chagrined to find an apparently learned writer claiming that some Illyrians possessed two pupils in each eye and could kill a man by glaring at him; and that "in the mountains of the land of India there are men who have the heads of dogs, and bark, and that they feed upon birds and wild animals." He notes that his own countryman, Pliny the Elder, had occasionally related similar nonsense in his monumental *Natural History* (*Historia Naturalis*). Reaching the limit of his endurance, Gellius says: "These and many other similar stories we read; but when we will write it down, it held us as worthless, not as useful writings, contributing nothing to the enrichment or adornment of life."[26]

His contempt was understandable. But perhaps Gellius was a bit too hard on Pliny and the other clueless scribblers. Man's knowledge of the natural world was more limited when compared with what we know today. He forgot that those writers did the best they could with the information available to them at the time. It is not that his predecessors were stupid. It was just that they did not have the benefit of reliable travel reports, scientific instruments, and consistent ways to disseminate knowledge. No doubt our remote descendants will laugh at our own pitiful ignorance of the solar system and its mysteries. I hope that, as they smile over our own printed absurdities, they will extend us some measure of sympathy.

Have we progressed in knowledge and understanding since Gellius's day? There are many paths of knowledge, and progress along all these paths is uneven. In science and technology, of course, we are far ahead of our ancestors. But in morals, the training of character, and virtue, the answer is much less certain. Our instrumentalities have become more advanced and complex, but our purposes and instincts remain the same as they always have been. Seen in this light, "progress" amounts to little else than new ways of achieving old goals. We fly around the world in dazzling times, and communicate with another at an instant; but have we really advanced beyond our ancestors in ethics and morals? We sense, somehow, that ancient and medieval man may have been wiser than we. He placed faith in the creations of his art, in spiritual values, and in beauty, rather than in the vulgar

---

[26] Haec atque alia istiusmodi plura legimus, sed com ea scriberemus, tenuit nos non idoneae scripturae taedium, nihil ad ornandum iuvandumque usum vitae pertinentis. *Noct. Att.* IX.4.12

worship of the latest gadgets. Medieval man believed he had already found "truth", and so could relax the ceaseless quest for knowing more about the universe.

Ancient historians, for example, often valued character and moral training over historical precision. They filled their books with imaginary speeches, epigrams, portents, and oracles, but there was a purpose behind these rhetorical flourishes. History was viewed as a teaching tool for character and moral development. In reading the ancient historians, one is conscious of their keen interest in proving some moral point, or illustrating some ethical virtue. This is why they wrote as they wrote. Thucydides, Polybius, Herodotus, Livy, Sallust, and Tacitus were certainly trying to show off their rhetorical skills, of course, but the recounting of historical events was meant to showcase a larger lesson. No modern writer can compete with, say, Plutarch, Livy, Quintilian, or Thomas a Kempis in moral training. We contrast this picture with that of our own day, where education overemphasizes factual knowledge, and completely neglects training in leadership, character, and morals. The results are obvious.

So is progress real? The French writer Bernard Le Bovier de Fontenelle (1657-1757), in his book *Digression sur les Anciens et les Modernes*, made some important observations in this regard. According to Fontenelle, there had been little or no progress since ancient times in poetry, literature, and art, but there had of course been considerable progress in science. Moreover, each nation goes through stages of development. In its infancy, a nation devotes itself to pure survival; later it cultivates the works of imagination, like poetry and art; and in its old age, it devotes itself to science and technology. For Fontenelle, progress was real and tangible. Only a fool would doubt that man had made tremendous strides toward his perfectibility across the centuries.

There is much to be said for this view. But perhaps I am that fool that Fontenelle speaks of. Looking at world history since the beginning of the twentieth century, it is now clear that science is neutral, rather than a gateway to utopia. It can kill us just as quickly as it can save us. Reading the works of ancient and medieval times, and learning about their societies, shows that perhaps imagination is more important than knowledge. Somewhere along the line, once the Age of Reason began in the sixteenth and seventeenth centuries, Western thought made a conscious decision to place its faith in science and technology, at the expense of its spiritual heritage. Mechanization trumped imagination.

We forgot the profound power of the imagination in opening the doors of perception. The rejection of our spiritual heritage has cut us off from other ways of perceiving the world, ways that do not involve machines or mechanical intermediaries. The Orientalist scholar Henry Corbin, who authored many books on Sufi mysticism, believed that the "imaginal world" was every bit as real as the physical world. Corbin's great work was describing the imaginative metaphysics of the mystic Ibn Arabi, and his work has been continued by the scholar William Chittick. For Corbin, the mystic's world of imagination was the "isthmus" or bridge that connected the corporeal world with the imaginal world of the Divine. Without a cultivation of the imagination, he held, a man could never hope to achieve true enlightenment. By polishing his soul, a man could achieve unique knowledge of the Divine Essence.

The West's great intellectual mistake since the Age of Reason, he believed, was to place all its faith in technology and turn its back on its Eastern spiritual legacy, which sprang from this "imaginal world." To be acquainted with the esoteric thought of Ibn Arabi is to be in awe of the awesome power of one man's imagination. Ibn Arabi's *Meccan Revelations* is an incredibly detailed cosmology of the mind and its universe, within the all-embracing theology of Islam. It would take two lifetimes for one man to scratch the surface of Ibn Arabi's thought. It is that profound. The dull, dry equations of the logician pale in comparison to the soaring power of Ibn Arabi's imaginative cathedrals. If the great mystic had ever met Bertrand Russell, he would have felt sorry for him, imprisoned within the walls of his cold, sterile equations and mathematical slight-of-hand. How inadequate Russell seems in comparison! Give me imagination, and keep your reason.

We cannot be sure Corbin was wrong in placing his faith in imagination over reason. All around us, I think, is evidence that the great thinkers of the West's Age of Reason (Bacon, Descartes, Hobbes, etc.) may have placed too much faith in logic and "reason" as a cure-all for man's woes. We have access to more and more, but seem to perceive less and less. We are drowning in information, but are more ignorant and unfulfilled than ever. The breakdown in discipline is a direct result of the abandonment of our ancient moral code, which sprang from imaginative religion. Every untried youth now believes himself fit to pass judgment on the intellectual heritage of several millennia.

Reason deceives as much as it enlightens. As man becomes more and more aware of the failures of reason in advancing his progress, it may be that the social pendulum will swing back towards a greater emphasis on character, faith, spirituality, and ethical progress. For progress to be real, we will eventually realize, it must take place across a wide spectrum of human knowledge, and this includes knowledge of the imaginative world. True and lasting progress means harnessing the imagination for creative endeavor, training the character and conduct to cope with the strains of earthly toil, and tapping into that hidden reservoir of potential that every man possesses, but few men use.

Even Gellius would have agreed with that assessment, I think.

12. THE MARCH OF WORLDLY WISDOM

We seek self-improvement in many areas: in physical fitness, language proficiency, travel, professional advancement, and in growth of character and worldly wisdom. Our premise is that development in all these areas makes us better and more successful men. It is relatively simple to measure our progress in the first five areas just listed. They are readily quantifiable fields of endeavor. Years ago, when I wanted to maximize my score on the Marine Corps physical fitness test, for example, I would work towards running three miles in eighteen minutes, doing eighty sit-ups in two minutes, and doing twenty pull-ups.

But how is it possible to "measure" our progress in developing character and wisdom? Is there any meaningful metric that can be used? The question is an important one. Without some method of regular self-examination, we will inevitably make things easier on ourselves. We will slide into complacency; advancement will come to a halt. We will become like the weight-lifter whose progress has reached a plateau, and then just fizzles out. There are some signs that can be used as indicators of progress in worldly wisdom. If you are aware of what they are, you will be more likely to notice them. As you continue your humanistic studies, and (more importantly) the flesh-and-blood school of hard knocks, you will begin to notice one or more of the following signs of maturing wisdom.

You are making regular contributions and additions to your philosophy of life. Wisdom accretes slowly, like mineral formations building in a cave from the steady dripping of water. As the poet Hesiod says in *Works and Days* (361-362): "If to a little you keep adding a little, and do so frequently, it will soon be a lot." You build your house of wisdom slowly, one timber and one shingle at a time.

You begin to notice connections between things (ideas, places, personalities, emotions, etc.) previously not perceived. Increasing wisdom and virtue opens doors of perception that were previously closed. Ultimately, all physical beings are connected in one way or another. The ability to perceive this, and to look beyond the façade of everyday life, is a sign of maturing wisdom.

You begin to lose enthusiasm for being around people without ambition or purpose. Abandoning people or things that add no value to your life is an important step in forward progress. Keeping company with dullards, fools, and dissolute people will bring you to ruin sooner or later.

Depressions of the mind or spirit become less frequent and more tolerable. The philosopher Plotinus, seeing that his pupil Porphyry was suffering from extreme depression, encouraged him to take an extended vacation in Sicily. The change in routine did him wonders, and accelerated his forward progress in Neoplatonism.

You are less and less disturbed by the foolishness, absurdities, and cruelties of the world. A major sign of progress is to maintain one's calm in the presence of the avalanche of nonsense which the world throws at us. I confess I need more improvement in this area.

Your style of discourse (in speaking and writing) begins to change. Refinement will inevitably become a feature of your discourse. As the gem becomes more polished and cut, it gleams more brightly.

You begin to lose your inflexibility in holding on to your cherished beliefs. What we once saw as doctrine, we begin to see as only one perspective. Certainty is the mark of a closed mind, and is murderous.

You no longer feel the need to convince or convert people to your position. People will arrive at the truth in their own time, and on the backs of their own horses. Losing an argument or debate with another man will mean nothing to you. Aristippus, after being verbally lashed by another man, said "I who have been beaten in an argument will have a better night's sleep than my victor."

You become less governed by your passions, and more governed by reflection and reason. Unformed spirits are slaves to their fear, greed, envy, and rage. As a man makes progress in acquiring wisdom, he shifts his focus from the baser passions to the milder, less serious ones. Advancement of wisdom takes the edge off the destructive passions. One example will illustrate this. Two of Renaissance Italy's most brilliant lights, Poggio Bracciolini and Lorenzo Valla, allowed themselves to be drawn into a bitter and extended quarrel. It was fought in the open, with all the acrimony which their powerful pens could muster. Another humanist, Francesco Filelfo, wrote to both of them, pleading them to cease and desist from their literary brawls. It is a masterful letter, and contained some pearls of wisdom:

> We are accustomed sometimes to desert our senses and follow the perturbations of our spirit; we do this type of thing when we are deceived by persuasion of others, who either hate us secretly or are desirous of revenge; they put out stimulations to insanity, which bring us to the most vehement agitation, so that we go against all human and divine directives, not thinking of our own dignity, but looking to do contumely and evil things against others...And what injury is it which forces you to such madness? It is enough that he who lies is unbalanced. This truly is the nature of a perturbed soul (with the violence, impetuosity, and the rage) that it cannot moderate itself...So he who is deprived of the

light of reason, as long as he lacks this, he neither understands anything clearly, nor rightly is able to judge.[27]

You become more focused on action, and less focused on excuses. The wise man knows that nothing in this world is attained without effort and struggle. He spends less time in fantasy, and more time in execution.

You begin to seek out other wise men and value their company. As Plutarch says, "And a young man improving in character instinctively loves nothing better than to take pride and pleasure in the company of good and noble men..." This is true not only of young men, but of men of all ages. The good seek out the good, and the wise seek out the wise.

You become more focused on attending to details. Carelessness and frivolity are feminine traits. The wise man, who seeks progress through study of philosophy, will begin to realize that this world is a serious place, requiring a certain sense of sobriety and application. The responsibilities of life should be embraced, not shirked.

You begin to see the unity of all things, and the love of this unity growing within you. As the philosopher and theologian Nicolas of Cusa says,

> Beauty of soul comes through love in devotion, and this that it is resolved in tears. It is like a fire that is applied to living wood, which burns one part while smoldering in another. And thus so it happens to a cold

[27] Letter to Poggio and Valla, 1453. *See* Cook, B. (ed.), *Lorenzo Valla: Correspondence*. Cambridge: Harvard University Press, 2013, p. 266-267.

soul...Therefore, love is the cause of order, and when it comes to an end, order does too.[28]

You become more and more drawn to the study of philosophy. If you care about the world and about yourself, then you care about philosophy. Its study will raise you to heights undreamed of. As the Roman writer Valerius Maximus says, in a brilliant aside in his *Memorable Doings and Sayings* (III.3):

> There is a powerful and steady militia of the spirit, influential through the written word, priestess of the timeless precepts of scholarship: philosophy. Who has received it in his heart, it drives off every useless and unbecoming affectation, confirms its edifice of solid virtue, and makes itself more powerful than fear and pain.

In the end, our powers of analysis can only do so much. There is an inescapable balance in life. The more difficult a goal is to achieve, the more worthwhile it will be. Acquiring worldly wisdom is the most difficult of all. You will mostly feel lost, bewildered, and confused. You will often feel like abandoning the pursuit altogether. But even in these moments, remember that you are progressing, even if you believe you are not. Watch for the signposts on the road, as I have listed them above, and continue on your journey. Allow others to help you. As the great Lorenzo Valla said, "To take pleasure in the success of the good and the wise falls only to him who is good and a lover of wisdom; this type of man, like all precious things, is rare and limited in number."[29]

––––––––––––––––––––

[28]Izbicki, Thomas (ed.), *Nicolas of Cusa: Writings on Church and Reform.* Cambridge: Harvard University Press, 2008, p. 473.
[29] Letter to Cardinal Tommaso Parentucelli, 1446. Cf. Cook, *supra* at 207.

You do not feel compelled to do things you do not wish to do. The developing mind will feel anguish at being forced to do things he does not want to do. He will feel anger or rage. Anger, properly understood, is essentially a form of pain; it is pain resulting from the inability to achieve one's ends. If we cannot change our environment, we can at least change ourselves. Through discipline and reflection, we can find a way to suture our own festering wounds, to salve our own burns, to alleviate the sting of painful knowledge with the blessings of consolation and guidance.

It is not good to say that someone else controls your emotional state. No one can "make" you behave one way or another. Thinking in this way empowers the other person, and renders the thinker helpless. And you are not helpless: no one can do anything to you that you do not permit them to do. Your identity is not conditioned on the approval of another. When you see someone behaving in an arrogant, haughty manner, think of this teaching anecdote by the Roman fabulist Phaedrus (IV.15):

> By the grace of Jupiter, the she-goats were able to obtain beards, just like the male goats. At this, the he-goats were full of indignation, afraid that the females would rival them in prestige and dignity. "Tolerate them," said the God, "and let them enjoy their empty honors and badges of your rank. It signifies nothing, as long as they do not equal you in masculine virtue."

As long as we remain centered in our masculine core, the unnatural behavior of another person should not be our concern. Our purpose is to seek a philosophy of life, a way of thinking, that will enable us to be lit by an inner light, a light that will guide us in this hostile modern environment; a philosophy that will enable us to draw sustenance and strength from ourselves, rather than from the approval of others. We travelers have spent a great deal of energy and effort to travel abroad. We travel here, and we travel there. But what about the inner journey? This is a profounder type of travel, one that will enable us to advance to ever-higher levels of consciousness, until we begin to approach true illumination. These are the journeys of the great mystics and poets of the past.

The mystic poet Farid ad-Din Attar (c. 1145-1220) in his great work *Discourse of the Birds*, believed that a sincere seeker could undertake a spiritual journey through six "valleys" or levels: Searching, Love, Knowledge, Detachment (from personal desires), Union (where he sees that all things are one), and Astonishment (losing sense of individual existence). Eventually, with persistence, he might be able to achieve the ultimate stage, Annihilation (of the self in the Divine). By going through these stages, Attar held, a seeker could become a "Perfect Man" who had the power of direct communion with the Divine. No soul is fully happy, says the pantheistic Attar, until it loses itself in this World Soul which emanates from the Divine. The only real religion was the search for such a union. Although Attar was severely attacked for his ideas, he confounded his critics by living a long and happy life.

Happier still was Saadi of Shiraz (c. 1184-1283), perhaps Persia's most beloved poet. For nearly thirty years he traveled all over the Near East and North Africa, experiencing all degrees of deprivation and poverty. He once complained that his shoes were in tatters, until he met a man without feet, and so "thanked Providence for the bounty." He fought in the Crusades, was captured by the Franks, released on ransom, and fell into a new kind of slavery after marrying the daughter of his ransomer. Eventually ridding himself of this servitude, he retired at age fifty to a small house in Shiraz, where he wrote poetry extolling the virtues of a simple life, animated by the sensual pleasures of physical love. The mystics were always careful to teach that the things of this world were illusory and fickle. To pursue them too rashly was to subject ourselves to inner torment and turbulence.

Ibn Arabi (c. 1165-1240) brought this idea to its fullest and most elaborate expression in his many esoteric volumes of prose and poetry. What the great mystics had in common was: a wide experience of travel, constant writing, a belief in their own inner light, spiritual exercises to achieve a level of enlightenment, a sense of humor, and a healthy enjoyment of worldly pleasure tempered with a knowledge that all such things were fleeting. We would do well to learn from them. The growth of wisdom involves a recognition that we should not feel bound to accept the expectations, limitations, and projections of others.

The poetry of Al-Mutamid (c. 1040-1095), Emir of Seville, is perhaps the last word on the folly of chasing the phantoms of the world. He led a life of combat, fighting at times both Christians and Moslems in Spain, yet never stopped writing verses. Eventually captured, he was brought in chains to Tangier where he lived until his death. One of his last poems expresses in a few lines what only long experience and true wisdom can ever hope to know:

> Do not woo the world too rashly, for behold,
> Beneath the painted silk and broidering,
> It is a faithless and inconstant thing.
> Listen to me, Mutamid, growing old.
> And we—that dreamed youth's blade would never rust,
> Who wished wells from the mirage, roses from the sand—
> Shall understand the riddle of the world,
> And put on wisdom with the robe of dust.[30]

---

[30] Quoted in Durant, Will, *The Age of Faith*, New York: Simon and Schuster, 1950, p. 307, and adapted from Mark Van Doren's *Anthology of World Poetry*.

13. ON HOW TO DISTINGUISH
A TRUE FRIEND FROM A FALSE ONE

That friendship is a precious thing is a truism no one disputes. The ancient Stoics went so far as to value it more highly than love between man and woman. Both Cicero and Seneca went to great lengths to praise the qualities of friendship, and its longevity, when compared with other human affections. We cannot be sure they were wrong. Yet the question of how to distinguish a true friend from a parasite is one worthy of reflection. Our relationships with our peers are vital to our well-being and survival; and time spent with false friends is time never to be recovered. Let us examine this question, and see if some features of the false friend can be identified.

The most dangerous type of false friend is the flatterer. He insinuates himself into our good graces by adroitly playing on our vanity and character flaws. Excessive praise casts doubt even on the sincerest friendship, and slowly corrupts the bonds of rectitude between men. Insincere flattery conceals itself in true friendship as a worm in an apple, and is not easily identified, being closely intertwined with fonder emotions. Since friendship is commonly the result of similar tastes between men, the parasitic false friend uses these common interests to gain an entry into the thresholds opened by candor. Just as a tick lodges itself in the ears of animals, so the parasitic friend also seeks out the ears of his patron, and uses his voice to gain entry into our sympathies. These are the primary traits of the parasitic friend:

The lack of a fixed character. The parasitic false friend has no fixed character of his own, and will adjust his opinions and positions with regard towards his environment. Like the organ-grinder monkeys of old, he will hop and gyrate to the tune of his patron, with a smile pasted on his face for our amusement. He shapes his own life on the lives of those he wishes to seduce. His method is to evaluate carefully the disposition and interests of his target, and then to build common ground with showy displays of sympathy to those interests.

The inability to speak the truth on relatively simple matters. The habits of dishonesty and mendacity, once acquired, are not easy for the parasite to shed. Such habits become permanent. They implant themselves in the consciousness of the flatterer. For this reason, you will find him denying the reality of even relatively unimportant things.

The seeking out of men of influence and position. No flatterer or parasite even sought to impress a lowly or impoverished man. Rather, he seeks to ingratiate himself with someone whose coattails he can ride. Surveying history, we note how frequently men of power and influence have been corrupted by parasites once they reach the heights of power. Why is this? Even men of sound judgment feel the isolations and pressures of responsibility, and long for an emotional release. The parasitic courtier, advisor, or sycophant provides this emotional release, at least in the short term. But the consequence is the degraded judgment and ailing faculties of the patron. Little by little, the patron becomes more isolated, more divorced from reality, and ultimately ruined.

Constant displays of subservience to his target. With true friends, there is little or no jealousy or rivalry. So a true friend will feel content, or apathetic, if his friend is more successful than he in some area. But the parasitic flatterer is ever mindful of his desire to be a minion to his target. He will make displays of his inferiority and subservience: his desire is always to remain "below" his target in ability or achievement. He wants not honest equality, but pandering subservience.

The desire to please above all else. A true friend will not hesitate to speak the truth, even though it may be unwelcome; but the parasite will place primary importance on the maintenance of good feeling. For this reason, he is very dangerous. The parasite's only goal is to echo the feelings and sentiments of his patron. Diseases of the body are often easily identified by their physical manifestations. But experience shows that afflictions of the soul are due to our vices, which are often hidden. The parasite feeds our vices and our delusions, thereby contributing to the spreading corruption of virtue within us. The proper diagnosis and correction of vice is hindered by a parasite's seductive flatteries.

His appearance in times of need. The false friend is especially attractive to us in times of hardship. We are at that point vulnerable, having been weakened in our resistance by the cruelties of fortune; and the flatterer has an instinctive sense of timing in this regard. While a true friend will not desert us in times of need, the parasitic false friend will hover about us, expressing his sympathies and seeking access to our hearts, but will never offer meaningful assistance.

His varying behavior with you and with others. Having no strong character himself, the parasite's behavior will vary greatly depending on whom he is talking to. He may praise you in private, and yet around others will offer subtle words of criticism to undermine your purposes. Filled with envy of others, he is unable to restrain his jealousies, and will swing from mood to mood depending on the whim of the moment. A true friend will never criticize or undermine you in the presence of others, as he knows that this would put both of you in a bad light.

His desire to inflame the worst instincts of his patron. The parasitic friend secretly despises his patron, despite his excessive flattery, and will cater to the worst vices of his target. A true friend will try to prevent harm from coming to him, and will do nothing to encourage his baser instincts. But the false friend, being full of malignity and insolence, takes secret pleasure in seeing his patron dragged through the mud of vice. These, then, are the hallmarks of the parasitic false friend. I have used the pronoun "he" in reference to such a person, but could just as easily have substituted "she." Both genders are equally capable of such behavior; and the danger may even be twofold when sexual intimacy is present in the equation. Lady MacBeths do exist in real life, if only we know where to look. Numberless men have been laid low, or brought down, by the taking into intimacy of women who subvert and destroy them. It is a fact as old as man on this earth.

Our best defense against the false friend is knowledge of ourselves. When we know ourselves, and do not allow our heads to become too puffed up with flattery, we will not allow the parasite entry into the corridors of our emotional sympathies. But how difficult to know oneself! Our powers of judgment are always skewed by secret prejudices, hidden passions, and heartfelt desires which cloak themselves in the garb of reason. We will spend our lives trying to know ourselves. As Seneca says,

Quis deus incertum est, habitat deus.[31]

Another defense is a thorough knowledge of men and their motivations. This, unfortunately, can only come from long experience and the reading of history. By becoming familiar with patterns of behavior, and the motivations behind them, we can develop some capacity to identify personality types that should be avoided. Our constant enemy is not the false friend, but those twin evils which the ancients called *vanitas* and *superbia*: vanity and pride, which blind our powers of identification, and close out our minds to the sagacity of good counsel. A major virtue of a good

---

[31] In every man a god dwells, but what type of god, we know not. *Epistulae XLI.2*

king, believed Cardinal Richelieu, was the ability to know *how to let himself* be served by his capable ministers.

But enough of these matters. We will say one more word regarding the qualities of true friends. A true friend will avoid the extremes: he will rarely use false flattery to manipulate his friend, and at the same time, he will be careful not to speak in a way that is too brutally honest. Sledgehammers make bad counselors. Constructive criticism should be delivered with delicacy, just as a bit of seasoning will enhance a dish, but not ruin it. Too harsh of a delivery of criticism will sew a lasting resentment into a friend's heart. A man can forgive nearly anything except an excess of honesty.

14. THE VALUE OF SINCERITY

The author of the first and most famous autobiography ever written was born in 354 A.D. in Tagaste, in Numidia, which had long been part Roman Africa. Augustine himself was likely a mix of Punic (i.e., Carthaginian), Numidian, and perhaps Roman ethnic stock, but we have no accurate image or bust of his likeness that has survived. He does not appear to have had much of a relationship with his father, but was close to his mother, St. Monica. She was a devout Christian, a new religion at the time, and it is likely that maternal influence may have played some role in forming the spiritual development of her famous son.

Augustine proved to be good student in rhetoric, philosophy, and Latin. His *Confessions* describes with enthusiasm how the reading of Cicero's work *Hortensius* (now lost) fired his passion for philosophy. He had to learn Latin as a second language; Punic, the old Carthaginian language (a Semitic tongue derived from Phoenecian) was still the speech of the common man in his region of North Africa. He pursued women readily, as any healthy young man would, and describes these experiences in general detail. He also relates his robbery of a pear orchard, showing that even saints could be rascals. After completing his schooling in Carthage he cohabited with a concubine, who soon bore him a son. Such was the custom of the time. Those who know the Roman Church only in its present form would be surprised at how the theologians of the early and medieval Church coexisted with the sexual mores of their eras.

One of the most touching parts of the *Confessions* is the passage where Augustine recounts his departure for Rome. In those days, any ambitious youth wanting to make his way in the world would at some point want to visit the Eternal City to polish off his higher education. His mother did not want him to go, afraid that he might die before being baptized. He pretended to agree with her, but then left secretly, a deception for which he expresses deep remorse:

> And so I lied to my mother, and this my own mother. So I got away from her. For this also you [God] have mercifully forgiven me, preserving me from the ocean's waters, then full of sordid things, and landing me safely at the water of your Divine Grace. As soon as I was cleansed with this, the tears of my mother's eyes should be dried up, with which she daily watered the ground under her face for me. [V.8]

He arrived in Rome, taught for a year, then moved to Milan for another teaching position. His mother eventually joined him. He also eventually replaced his mistress for a young wife, but not before enjoying the affections of another woman. His intellectual development was volatile: at various times he flirted with Manicheism and Neoplatonism, but listening to some sermons of Ambrose, combined with his own reading, won him over to Christianity. In a ceremony with his friend Alypius and his son (from his former mistress) Aeodatus, he was baptized and entered the faith.

From this point Augustine embarked on a remarkable career of teaching, organization, and writing. It is nothing short of amazing that this man, so instrumental in laying the structural and theological foundations of the early Church, found the time to write so voluminously. His collected writings fill many hundreds of pages, in the clearest, simplest, and most lucid Latin prose since Caesar. Two of his works—his autobiography and his *City of God*—are among the classics of world literature.

Reading the *Confessions* is a deeply personal experience. Although arguably the most famous autobiography written, it is different in that it is a spiritual testament. One historian called it a "100,000 word act of contrition." And it is. Augustine addresses it directly to God, and it reads like a series of meditations on his past. What strikes the reader, and impresses him the most, is the utter sincerity of the work. There is no false modesty, no hedging, no passive-aggressive asides, and no attempt to dodge or rationalize. There are only the heartfelt words of a deeply religious yet accessible and human figure. Somehow the pure honesty of the work wins us over completely, and we are carried along by the meandering stream of his tender prose:

> Let not the proud speak ill of me now. I ponder on the price of my soul (*pretium meum*), and do eat and drink, and give alms to the poor. And desiring poverty myself, desire to be filled by Him, amongst those that eat, and are satisfied. And they will praise the God who seeks him. [X.43]

The overall impression given is that of a pious man trying to help other men through the spiritual wilderness which he had to traverse before finding a belief system that gave him peace. What is shocking is to remember that this testament was written by Augustine when he was a forty six year old bishop. His frank descriptions of his seductions, thefts, wanderings, jealousies, and theological doubts must have seemed incredible to his contemporaries. Here is a theologian who has stripped himself down before the world, and revealed himself in a way that none had before or has since. The *Confessions* has an overtly mystical tone to it, which reminded me of the writings of the medieval Islamic mystics. If you have to read only one religious-themed book, this is the one to read. The Loeb Classical Library has just released a wonderful new translation, along with the original Latin text. Augustine's Latin is clear and usually direct, and well within the reach of the ambitious student of the language with a few years of study under his belt.

Augustine's later years were tempestuous. The early centuries of the Church were afire with controversies and disputes, and the new faith sought to hammer out its ideology among numerous competing heresies and visions. Politically, the world was also turbulent. The Roman Empire was collapsing, and the Church was doing its best to fill the vacuum left by the feeble authority of the Caesars. When the Vandals surged through Spain and moved into North Africa, Augustine was still a bishop there, with authority over the region. As the Vandal invasion progressed and the people began to suffer, he showed his physical courage by ordering other bishops not to abandon their posts, but to stay and take care of the populace. He led by example, remaining himself at Hippo. He died during the siege of his city at the age of seventy six.

His influence was immense. In an age of war, poverty, and rising barbarism, his words and teachings had an appeal that is difficult for us to grasp fully now. The classical world was evolving into the medieval world, and the mood of the times was to turn away from the old gods, the old rationalism, and the old ways, and seek something that would answer the needs and wants of the simple man. Men had become tired of the pursuits of temporal vanity, and longed for an ethic that would provide certainty and comfort amid the chaos, and a hope for eternal life after death. The new faith promised what the old religions could not: a chance to share in the fountain of grace offered by God's only son, who sacrificed himself for the redemption of every man. No other religion of those turbulent centuries could match Christianity's ethical and moral teachings. His *Confessions* is a monument to that ethic, and the voice of the age. It is the sincerest book ever written.

15. EASTER ISLAND'S COLLAPSE

Jared Diamond's book *Collapse: How Societies Choose To Fail Or Succeed* is a collection of case studies of societies that were unable or unwilling to correct certain flaws which ultimately led to their destruction. The examples studied include the Anasazi culture of North America, the Vikings of Greenland, the Mayans, and even modern Rwanda. But for me the most haunting example of collapse was Easter Island. Diamond explains how the decline and collapse played out in great detail, taking advantage of the most current scientific research. The resulting story is unforgettable, and drives home an important lesson.

When most people think of Easter Island, of course, they imagine the great monoliths erected there by the inhabitants centuries ago. Seen today, the island is nearly bare, with no trees over ten feet tall. It was not always so: the island was once a thriving ecosystem, with extensive forests, numerous bird species, and a wealth of vegetable species. When humans first arrived there about A.D. 900, it was densely forested, and was capable of sustaining numerous tribes and a relatively high population. When the first Europeans "discovered" the island in the 1720s, they found it very sparsely populated, the inhabitants reduced to a pitiable state of existence, and the landscape denuded of trees. What had happened?

The scientific evidence makes it clear that overexploitation of resources by the natives set in motion a chain of events that pushed the inhabitants over the brink. Trees were an important resource for the islanders: they used them for cremation, construction of statutes, and habitations. But the islanders were unable—or unwilling—to manage their natural resources in ways that ensured their continued renewal. Gradually, perhaps nearly imperceptibly, the resources began to dwindle. As deforestation proceeded, animal life became extinct or went elsewhere. Crop yields plummeted. Native plants, birds, and animals melted away.

The islanders began to compete with each other more and more fiercely for an ever-declining volume of natural resources; vendettas multiplied, intertribal warfare flared, and a pall of hostility and fear descended on the island. As the trees vanished, the islanders were unable to build boats to escape to other islands: they became trapped in their own hell, doomed to fight each other in perpetuity for the last crumbs that the denuded could offer. Eventually the islanders began to starve, and feed—literally—off each other. As wild meats became unavailable, and escape off the island became impossible, the natural consequences followed. Cannibalism stalked the island. The folklore that has come down to us, and the archaeological record, make this clear. Perhaps they compensated for their misery by focusing more and more on the empty ritual of building and raising statutes, as their life-blood melted away. It is an unsettling picture, impossible to forget.

Diamond poses a question worthy of some reflection. He asks, "As an islander cut down the last tree, what would he have been thinking?" He notes that modern analogues offer a possible answer: "It's about jobs, not trees!" or "God will take care of it", or "Next year will be better!" Just as many today are in denial about resource depletion and global warming, so we can imagine that the ancient Easter Islanders may have had some soothing, face-saving explanation for why they could not take action to avert disaster.

Denial is a curious thing. We choose to ignore the problems that confront us, because doing so involves some degree of self-examination. I have often noticed that when people or businesses are confronted with problems, they will continue to do the same thing over and over again, even when such a course of action has demonstrably failed. In some cases, speedy and decisive action may have saved a situation that was allowed to degrade to the point of no return. And then it becomes too late for remedial action. Why does this happen? I think the answer is that on some level, people, organizations, or nations make a conscious choice. They choose to fail or to succeed. Faced with a fork in the road, we are all forced to make a choice. And the truth seems to be that some people actually prefer to fail. Perhaps failure validates some hidden prejudice, or secret self-destructive impulse, that they have; or perhaps they find it impossible to extricate themselves from the situation in any other way.

I remember some dialogue from the 1997 film *The Edge*, which was written by David Mamet. In the film, the characters become stranded in the Alaskan wilderness after a plane crash, and are forced to make their way out back to civilization. The Anthony Hopkins character asks the Alec Baldwin character what people lost in the wilderness truly die of. They die of shame, Hopkins says. He means that, overwhelmed by despair and shame at their predicament, they fail to mobilize and do the things necessary that might save themselves. They simply lie down and die. The analogy is an effective one.

But it still is baffling to outside observers to see a situation, that could clearly have been remedied, continue to spiral downward for no good reason. Call it the power of the irrational, which is a constant attendant to human affairs. Easter Island's collapse highlights the power of choice in mankind's affairs. For me, it is a reminder that we, and we alone, retain the power to sketch the contours of our destiny. There is no shame in survival.

16. JOHN PAUL JONES

The daring exploits of John Paul Jones during the American Revolutionary War earned him international fame as America's first great naval hero. A Scotsman by birth, he possessed all the sternness, willpower, and volcanic temperament of his people, qualities which made him a formidable commander on the high seas; but like most great men, his virtues contained the seeds of his faults. After the war ended in 1783, Jones found it difficult to accommodate himself to the politics and maneuverings of the peacetime military. His fighting skills and experiences suddenly counted for little, as the new country proceeded to demobilize and concentrate on commerce. A fighting admiral, he could not suffer fools or endure the subtleties of diplomacy, and he was at pains to appease the bureaucrats in Congress to secure a position for himself as head of the fledgling U.S. Navy. When funding and ships failed to materialize as promised, Jones felt insulted and unappreciated. Disappointed with his prospects in America, he sailed for Europe, never to return.

He found eventual employment, incredibly, with the Russian Empire, and became a favorite of Catherine the Great, Slavicizing his name to Pavel de Zhoves. But even there, his career prospects eventually dried up, and he found himself in Paris in 1790. He died two years later, exhausted and embittered, and still chasing his ambitions. His death was unreported in the United States, and his funeral was attended by a scant few close friends. A knight permanently in search of a liege lord to serve, he had found little rest while he was alive, and he had been unable to recast his identity in a way suitable for a peacetime life. In the end, he realized that this world, and everything in it, is a maya of transitory phantoms, melting into the swirling mists of our consciousness.

A century passed. At the dawn of the twentieth century, the United States had been transformed from a provincial backwater to an industrial powerhouse. Interest had been reawakened in the heroes of the Revolutionary War. Historians gradually began to realize that John Paul Jones had had a remarkable career, and was the country's first great fighting admiral. But no one seemed to know what had happened to him. Jones had died at the height of the French Revolution, and in the upheaval and turbulence of the period, records had been lost or remained fragmentary and incomplete. Where he had lived, and the location of his final resting place, no one knew or cared to know. The American ambassador to France, Horace Porter, was a quiet and industrious man with a keen interest in naval history. He was personally outraged that an American national hero had been so cruelly served by his adopted nation, and he resolved to put the matter right. In 1899 he embarked on a personal quest to locate Jones and return him to America for a proper burial. He was acting purely on his own, as a private citizen.

But where to start? He found that the death certificate had been consumed by a building fire in 1871. Luckily someone had made a copy of it in 1859, and this copy had been hidden away in a mountain of records in an old archives building. According to the document, Jones's death occurred on July 18, 1792. Other documents yielded other clues. A letter from one of Jones's friends who had attended the funeral mentioned that the coffin had been encased in thick lead "in case the United States, which he had essentially served and with so much honor, should claim his remains, they might be more easily moved." Porter was shocked to discover that the American government had not even paid for Jones's funeral expenses. This burden had fallen to a friend of the admiral's named M. Simoneau, who had paid roughly 500 francs for Jones's leaden coffin, the embalming of the body in alcohol, and the outer wooden coffin. Moved to pity and shame by the revelation, he tried to find a descendant of Simoneau's to reimburse, but to no avail.

At this point Porter had to resort to guesswork, his remaining leads having run cold. He guessed that foreign non-Catholics in Paris such as Jones would most likely have been buried in the St. Louis Cemetery. A search of the graveyard records found that they were fragmentary and incomplete, a likely consequence of the ferocity and upheaval of the French Revolution. The missing records miraculously turned up in a Paris library, and Porter was back on the trail of his prey: the records proved that Jones had indeed been buried at the St. Louis Cemetery. But further problems remained. The cemetery had been sold in 1796 by France's revolutionary government to a dodgy private building contractor named M. Phalipeaux, who then (probably illegally) swept away the headstones and erected commercial buildings on the site.

Porter was further disturbed to find that the site later had become a dumping ground for the cadavers of horses and dogs. Porter approached the owners of the property (today located at the corner of Rue Grange-aux-Belles and Rue des Ecluses St. Martin) to request permission to conduct some excavations on the land. The owners were not favorably disposed to negotiate on reasonable terms. Word had leaked out that a wealthy American was poking about in grungy Parisian back-lots, looking for old bones, with the predictable result that local imagination stoked the fires of avarice. They demanded so much money from Porter that he thought the best course of action would be to walk away and let the matter sit for some time. He then quietly re-approached the owners after twenty four months, and explained that his resources were limited, and that the object of his quest had little value beyond that which might be derived from national honor. An agreement was eventually reached, and shafts were sunk on the land in search of the admiral's casket.

Eventually, after probing the entire property and sifting through numerous animal skeletons, five caskets of lead were recovered. All of them save one were marked with identification plates. The unmarked one, Porter concluded, had to be Jones's casket; during the chaos of the French Revolution, no proper engraver could be found. The casket was opened, and a well-preserved corpse was found wrapped in linen and straw, which matched old portraits and a marble bust of Jones. A detailed examination done at the Paris School of Medicine established beyond doubt that the body was that of John Paul Jones. President Theodore Roosevelt, hearing of the recovery of the remains of Jones in Paris, was moved by the pathos of the story. With his usual flair for the dramatic, Roosevelt decided to send a squadron of warships to carry the body back to Annapolis, Maryland for proper burial. Porter himself faded from history. His tenacity had made the recovery of the body possible, but he was never reimbursed by the U.S. government for his efforts. Time heals old wounds, and inflicts new ones.

Memorial services were held on April 24, 1906. President Roosevelt spoke the following words:

> Remember that no courage can ever atone for the lack of preparedness which makes the courage valuable. And yet if the courage is there, its presence will sometimes make up for other shortcomings; while if with it are combined other military qualities, the fortunate owner becomes literally invincible.

Roosevelt chose April 24 as the day for commemorative services. On that very day, 138 years before, Jones had captured the British man-of-war *Drake*. In triumph and pity, the remains of America's first great maritime warrior were entombed in their final resting place, while mourners prayed for the repose of his soul. After 130 years, the man who had only just begun to fight finally lowered his spyglass, sheathed his cutlass, and entered the Pantheon of Heroes with a measure of silent dignity. It was without doubt his greatest victory.

17. SOME GUIDANCE ON FOREIGN LANGUAGE LEARNING

One of the key steps needed in any man's development is the learning of foreign languages. Unfortunately, like so many critical skills, there are many differences of opinion on how to go about accomplishing this goal. Many men have convinced themselves that the goal is beyond their reach, when in fact they have not been pursuing it in an efficient way. I wanted to share my own tips and thoughts on what has worked for me over the years.

No one is going to help you. There is a pervasive myth that being around native speakers will enable you to learn by osmosis. Or, men think that a native speaker girlfriend will solve all their problems. Not so. You have to do the grunt work in the beginning, and native speakers, even if they may be your friend or lover, often do not have the patience to listen to you flummox about in their language. And in many cases, in foreign countries, people will be more interested in using you for English practice. Of course, interaction with natives is critical, but you need to be realistic about what it will and will not do for you. Success comes when you realize that you have to fight for this goal alone.

Conventional classroom language classes are better than nothing, but are usually the least efficient way. The reason is simply that they are too rudimentary. They are not difficult enough. They use passive, old fashioned instructional methods. They are also too infrequent. You need daily contact with the language, something that classroom work does not provide. Instead, focus on being a self-learner.

Choose your books, workbooks, and recordings very carefully. Most of the courses on the market today are simply too easy. You need something that is going to make serious demands on your cognitive abilities if you want to improve. I have found that the resources offered by the academic presses of Georgetown, Yale, Cambridge, and Oxford to be very good. Whichever courses you choose, they should have certain things in common:

1. It should contain a large number of dialogues for a variety of situations: basic social situations, doctor, work, employment, renting, music, dating, repairing vehicle, discussing politics, health, education, current events, etc. There must be recordings with the materials. Books with no recordings are not worth much. You need to hear the dialogues and memorize them. Repeat them aloud. Converse with yourself. Repetition is critical, and you need to hear yourself speaking. I prefer courses that employ the "natural language" method: only the target language is used in instruction. No English is used. You need to begin training yourself to use the language right from the beginning.

2. The books should be well made in order to hold up to frequent use, and should have ample margins to write notes. Every word you don't know should be written down and spoken aloud. Keep a separate composition book to write the words again, and review them frequently.

3. At the intermediate and advanced stages, you should be using good readers with ample explanatory notes. A good reader will have selections of articles from the popular press, history, folklore, education, art, etc. You need to be exposed to a variety of vocabulary.

4. Buy a variety of courses. No one single course is enough. The variety will do you good, and help reinforce previous learning.

5. Besides good books and recordings, you will need a good reference grammar at the intermediate and advanced stages. Notice I did not say at the beginning stages. Trying to learn too

107

much grammar in the beginning will only slow you down. Remember, the goal is to learn the language, not to learn about the language.

6. Flash cards are all right, as a supplement in your down time, with certain caveats. You should have a set with about 2500 of the most commonly used verbs. (Verbs are more important than nouns). But to be worth anything, they should have an illustrative sentence on one side of the card. Say the sentence out loud, always. Memorization occurs in context, not in isolation. I like the cards made by Tuttle Publishing Company, which I believe is an Australian company.

7. Emotions affect performance. Be aware that "affective filters" can block your performance. Studying should be done at a time when you are relaxed and refreshed, not when you're tired.

8. Don't worry too much about different dialects. Just learn the standard version of whatever language you are studying. Specialists and linguists like to make a big fuss about how there are different dialects of whatever language you are studying. Many languages also have a feature called "diglossia" where there are different "versions" of the language used in formal and informal contexts. And they are correct, but they also like to make things harder than they need to be. Focusing on it too much can hinder your progress. Just learn the standard version of the language. You can pick up the dialect versions later, once you have a baseline of competence. So, for example, don't worry about learning some dialect of Italian, just learn the standard literary variety, at least in the beginning.

9. Older books are often better than the newer ones. This is not always true, of course, but you'd be surprised how good some of the stuff made in the 1960s is, compared with now. I also think computer-based courses are generally worthless.

10. Ask native speakers to correct you. Instant correction on the spot will help to prevent what are called "fossilized errors", or errors that become embedded in your speaking style.

11. Take a break every few months. The mind needs time to rest and let the material "gel" in your head. You will find that coming back after a brief layoff will enable you to be stronger and better than before.

12. Daily commitment is necessary for cementing the structures and patterns of the language in your long-term memory. You need to be working *at least* 30 minutes per day, every day, for a few years. If you can't handle this commitment, then you will not be successful.

If you are studying more than one language at a time, make sure you use different desks or tables in your house or apartment. I learned this technique in a biography of Sir Richard Burton, an amazing 19th century British explorer and linguist. He had a separate desk in his house for each language he studied. The technique works: the mind tends to associate each different place with what is studied there. This speeds learning and prevents "linguistic interference" where one language interferes with another.

13. You need regular exposure to soap operas, movies, podcasts, cable TV, or internet. Subtitling is a good thing if you can get it. Satellite "free-to-air" TV is also good. The internet has made the old option, shortwave radio, almost totally obsolete.

14. Do not settle into a rut. Language learning is like working out. You are going to hit plateaus and do not want the mind to settle into a comfortable rut. Every few months, shake yourself up and mix the pot a little. You should be shocking your system periodically to prevent monotony and drudgery from sapping your cognitive freshness.

15. Memorize a short story, anecdote, fable, or poem. And be able to deliver it flawlessly. In the old days, language learners memorized large volumes of text in the target language. It helps cement structures in your brain. But it is also a good way to charm native speakers. Being able to rattle off a whole story or fable in the target language can be very impressive.

16. In the intermediate and advanced stages, it is a good idea to go to a major news website in your target language and print off short one page articles on current events, economics, health, culture, or whatever, and then translate them. Keep a book to write down all unknown vocabulary. Say the article out loud. This will keep you current on idioms, structures, and popular culture.

17. Expect plateaus, and do not be derailed or frustrated by them. The most common plateaus are:

a. Limited vocabulary (find yourself using the same words over and over again)

b. Fossilized errors (making the same mistakes so often that they become part of your conversational routine).

c. Not knowing enough grammatical constructions to express yourself fully.

As I said above, you just have to fight through plateaus. Keep plowing forward, keep up the daily grind. Remember that the people who succeed in learning are the ones willing to put in the sweat. Language learning can be a very tedious grind at times, but you should be motivated to do it. The rewards are priceless. When you find yourself in a foreign land interacting with native speakers and shedding your old skin, you will know without doubt that you have spent your time wisely.

18. FIRING MACARTHUR

I have long been a student of the Korean War. It has many compelling dimensions to it—political, military, social, and diplomatic—and any one of these facets makes it a fruitful field for study. One revealing episode that occurred during the war has come to stand for the principle of ultimate civilian control over the military. This was the removal of General Douglas MacArthur by President Truman. It is difficult today to grasp fully the awe in which MacArthur was held by the American public in the early 1950s. He had been in the public eye in one way or another since the early 1930s, and had cultivated his public image in such a way as to appear as military genius sitting atop Mount Olympus. A major figure in the defeat of Japan in the Pacific in the Second World War, he had remained in Japan as an administrator, ruling the country with Oriental remoteness and absolutism. Long accustomed to doing what he wanted, and adept at insubordination, he had been indulged by his superiors for so long that he had come to believe himself beyond scrutiny. His nominal bosses, the Joint Chiefs of Staff, were actually afraid of him; and MacArthur, an expert political infighter, knew how to keep them off balance with a mixture of tantrums and veiled threats.

He was a man of contradictions. As superintendent of West Point, he proved himself an efficient administrator and progressive reformer; in the Second World War, he showed his tactical brilliance on many occasions; and in Korea, his amphibious landing at Inchon turned the tide of the war and came within an ace of winning it. Charismatic, highly intelligent, and brave, he could also be vain, spiteful, pathologically insecure, and jealous of colleagues and subordinates.

MacArthur's gamble at the Inchon landings in 1950 had been brilliantly successful. He had pulled off a masterstroke, outflanking the North Koreans who just weeks earlier had had the US and South Koreans boxed into a steadily shrinking perimeter around Pusan. Against all the naysayers, he had triumphed; the North Koreans, in full retreat, seemed now close to complete collapse. As he moved into North Korea and plunged northward, he committed two unforgiveable military blunders: he divided his forces for separate northward advances, and he refused to listen to intelligence reports that China was preparing an all-out invasion in support of its beleaguered North Korean ally.

But the Chinese did enter the war, and with both feet. MacArthur's forces were sent reeling back down the peninsula. The US Army came close to full collapse; the US Marines, with their superior discipline and cohesiveness, were only with great difficulty able to extricate themselves from the frozen wastes of the Chosin Reservoir. The changing fortunes of war had deeply shocked MacArthur. His carelessness and vanity had been responsible for the disaster, yet he refused to accept any measure of blame.

Losing the war on the ground and increasingly divorced from reality, he reverted to living in his fantasies. MacArthur's public statements became more and more provocative. He began to challenge openly US policy in the Far East: he threatened to "unleash" Chiang Kai-Shek in Taiwan on the communist Chinese mainland, and to widen the war beyond Korea. In increasingly bombastic and insubordinate public statements, he appeared to endorse to use of atomic bombs on China and the Soviet Union, and, even worse, edged towards suggesting the inadequacy of President Truman's leadership. Repeated attempts to admonish him and rein him in came to nothing. Like a spoiled child who had been indulged too often, MacArthur's behavior by 1951 had become nearly impossible to correct. Thus was the stage set for one of the most dramatic confrontations in the history of American politico-military affairs. The National Security Agency (NSA), newly created in 1947, routinely monitored communications of both friends and foes of the US from its monitoring station at Atsugi Air Base near Tokyo. Intercepts of MacArthur's conversations with foreign diplomats (mainly Spain and Portugal) demonstrated his inclination to widen the war outside Korea, so as to destroy the communist Chinese and chasten the USSR. When Truman was briefed on MacArthur's machinations with foreign diplomats, he was furious. It simply could not be tolerated. Even without these secret conversations, Truman had enough evidence of his general's insubordination (MacArthur's professionally suicidal public statements questioning US policy in Korea) to justify his sacking of MacArthur. He had finally forced Truman's hand.

All that remained was to notify MacArthur of his firing. To spare MacArthur embarrassment, it was decided to have a courier quietly hand-deliver the relief notice to the general's home in Tokyo. Everyone involved was sworn to secrecy. But somehow the message traffic got stalled, and then a loose-lipped official in Tokyo leaked the story to a reporter. Panic seized the Truman administration. It was feared that, if MacArthur got wind of his firing before being officially notified, he might make some sort of grandstanding speech to the press to further sabotage US policy in Korea.

Truman's only option was to preempt MacArthur by calling a press conference at one o'clock in the morning on April 11, 1951. Truman's announcement to the press was terse and resolute. "With deep regret" he declared that he believed MacArthur was "unable to give his whole-hearted support" to US policies in Korea. "For that reason I repeat my regret at the necessity for the action I feel compelled to take in this case." It was unfortunate that these circumstances—rousing reporters in the dead of night for a press conference--made the firing of MacArthur seem an impetuous and irrational act by Truman, which was in fact untrue.

The comic opera continued, and had one final act. MacArthur found out about his sacking in the worst way possible: a colleague heard it on the radio, who then called MacArthur's wife to inform her that her husband had been "relieved of all his commands." When the general himself finally got the official notice, he hugged his wife and said, "Jeannie, we're going home at last."

On his return to the US, MacArthur addressed a joint session of Congress with a masterpiece of oratory. He then went on a speaking tour of America. Feeling ran high against Truman, who had already been deeply unpopular on account of the little-understood Korean War. Truman wisely lay low until the storm passed, but he never quite recovered from the incident. As time has given us some perspective on the matter, it is clear that Truman's removal of MacArthur was an act of deep courage, taken under circumstances that Truman knew would expose himself to retaliation from MacArthur's political friends in Congress. But MacArthur had had it coming, and he knew it. He had stonewalled on his orders, had expressed open contempt for his president, had conspired against his nation's policies behind the scenes, and had failed on the battlefield. In the history of armed conflict, no removal of a wartime general has been as justified, and as necessary. It is a leadership lesson that resonates with us today, wherever lawful authority is fundamentally challenged by the pungent brew of charisma, hubris, and guile. So the fates of men and nations may hinge on the denouement of these fateful contests.

In May 2014, I was in Tokyo. I had not been there since 2008, and wanted to get a fresh perspective on the city. In the morning, I would walk from my hotel along the pathway bordering the Imperial Palace, on my way to the Ginza. MacArthur's old building, the Dai Ichi, was still there, having been bought by an insurance company for some such financial purpose. Walking through the lobby, I could see no sign that this was once the seat of power in Japan during the Occupation period. The people coming and going in the lobby likely had no idea who MacArthur even was. Scarcely any trace of the once-supreme shogun remained. All that remained were vague and indistinct memories. *Sic transit gloria mundi.*

19. A GREAT PHYSICIAN

Greatness is more often the result of years of patient labor than the phosphorescence of a singular incident. Gradually but persistently, like the drips of water falling in a cave and accreting mineral formations, the labors of the great man may take many years to produce results. But when the results to come, they can move awe in the soul. We, the spectators, stand in wonder at the finished products, but forget the painstaking toil that produced them. Overnight success, someone once said, usually takes about ten years. In fact, it usually takes a lot longer than that.

Andreas Vesalius came from a Brussels family with a notable history in the medical profession. By all accounts, as a boy he was consumed with a passion for the natural world, and soaked up all available information on biology, anatomy, and medicine. His special passion was dissection, for which he developed a prodigious talent. He showed signs of genius at an early age: at twenty two years old he was able to lecture to pupils in Latin, and was able to read the medical works of Galen in the original Greek. Medical science in Europe at the time was held hostage by the ancient texts of Galen, Celsus, and Aristotle, and by traditional theological disapproval of anatomical research. Galen's work, although brilliant in its day, had not kept pace with the advancement of learning in the intervening millennium. Vesalius found the slavish devotion to his texts at Louvain schools to be suffocating. Secretly, he and friends prowled the charnel houses for cadavers to bring into the lecture halls and vivisect. He suffered no fools and, like many great men, found it hard to keep his passions under control. He soon found it prudent to leave

Louvain and relocate to Padua, Italy, where he received his doctorate; in 1537, the Venetian authorities appointed him professor of surgery and anatomy at the University of Padua. He was only twenty three years old.

Vesalius kept meticulous and voluminous notes of his researches over many years, a fact that would be of inestimable value in the next phase of his life in Italy. From 1541 to 1543, while working with colleagues on a complete revision of the medical texts of Galen, he became more and more aware that an entirely fresh perspective was needed. Traditional ways of thinking would have to be thrown out completely. Great moments in science seem to come when a pioneer--either through a flash of insight or simply out of desperation-- finally jettisons the old paradigms and adopts an entirely new model. So Copernicus and Kepler finally realized that the Ptolemaic orbital systems could not be reconciled with the observed astronomical data; and so Max Planck, in desperation at his inability to explain the nature of blackbody radiation, finally adopted a quantum-based mathematical model that could explain his observations. Vesalius had reached a point of no return. Regardless of the cost, he resolved to drag the science of anatomy, kicking and screaming, into the modern world. The result was the greatest medical work ever written.

In 1543, at the age of twenty nine, Vesalius published in Switzerland the first edition of *De Humani Corporis Fabrica* (On the Structure of the Human Body). No one had ever seen anything like it before. Printed in 663 glorious folio pages, it contained nearly 300 original woodcuts which by themselves could have stood independently as works of art. Many of the engravings were made with Vesalius's own hand. Here was finally revealed the intricate and detailed structure of every part of the human body, in a methodical, confident way that was staggering in its breadth and scope.[32] Everything was based on original first-hand research, with no reliance on, or allowance made, for hearsay. It is perhaps difficult for us now, several centuries removed, fully to realize how revolutionary his book was. But we must remember that the entire basis of modern medicine rests on a detailed factual understanding of how the body works. And Vesalius's labors showed the way. For the first time was described the ventricles of the heart, the operation of the veins, the uterus, the liver, the brain, the skeletal system and bone structure, and the function of the other internal organs. He had mapped the body with the same masterly thoroughness that Johannes Kepler described the orbits of the planets. And he laid the observational groundwork that later generations would build on.

Expectedly, he was resented by older colleagues and the theological authorities whom he had no use for. Like many great pioneers, he made enemies everywhere who feared the overthrow of the existing paradigms. Some academics tried to explain Galen's errors by claiming that the human body had "changed" since antiquity. In frustration at the pettiness of his peers, Vesalius left Italy and took a position as medical advisor at the court of Charles V of Spain, where he found himself a foreigner at odds with the native Spanish physicians. It is not unlikely that he was under suspicion by the Inquisition, which never forgave his refutation of scripture with applied science. He issued an expanded second edition of the *Fabrica* in 1555, which contained even more original research.

---

[32] The original woodblock engravings, lovingly preserved by Vesalius in his lifetime, were lost after his death. They were rediscovered by accident at the University of Munich's library in 1893. During the Second World War, they were destroyed in a bombing raid. So the folly of man obliterates the wisdom of the ages.

His powers remained unequalled. In 1562, the king's only son suffered a concussion and serious head trauma from a fall. Vesalius recommended a brain operation which involved opening the skull, which was rejected with horror by the king's sycophantic entourage. As the prince neared death, Charles finally consented to let Vesalius perform the surgery, which was completely successful. Like many men of genius, he had the faults of his formidable powers. Far ahead of his contemporaries, he found it difficult to extend forbearance to foolery, and impossible to leave ignorance unanswered. It was in his nature. His flame burned brightly, yet with tragic brevity. Men of action often find it difficult to relax, and to know when to stop. For reasons that are not clear, he eventually left Spain to go on a pilgrimage to Jerusalem. He reached the holy city, but was shipwrecked off the island of Zante in Greece on his return voyage in 1564 and died of exposure. He was only fifty years old.

Vesalius's mapping of the human body laid the observational groundwork for later discoveries by Servetus and Sir William Harvey. As a physician and scientist, he had no equal. But he paid a high price for his genius. Working under difficult conditions and in hostile environments, he developed a protective shield of curtness that often wounded his friends and colleagues. He was generous to a fault with his friends, and had none of the vindictiveness or petty jealousies that afflicted some of his peers. Hardly thirty years old, he was able to dethrone the Galenic view of medicine and anatomy that had held sway in Europe for over a thousand years. In an age where the boundary between art and experimental science was often indistinct, his *Fabrica* remains a masterpiece of both. An outsider in many environments, he did his best to balance his ambitions with the intolerance of the age he lived in. He exhausted himself in his lifelong pursuit of knowledge, yet elevated his patient labors with the inspiring dignity of a scholar and the courageous objectivity of a true scientist.

20. ILLUSIONS AND DELUSIONS

Recently I went to a movie theater for the first time in a while. Before the coming attractions rolled, there appeared on the screen a public service announcement in which the American president, vice-president, and assorted A-list actors (Daniel Craig, Benicio Del Toro, and Steve Carrell) lectured us solemnly on the supposed problem of "non-consensual sex" on college campuses. It was a remarkable spectacle. One would think that these political and cultural figures were speaking of a topic critical to the survival of the human species, so grave was the tone. I began to think more and more about this little announcement as I left the theater, and how incredible it was that the head of state and vice president of the world's most powerful nation actually had taken the time and effort to advise the public—with all the other varied issues on their agendas—about a problem that was entirely imaginary. Even I, jaded with long experience with American male groveling before the altar of feminine frivolity, was taken aback. I could hardly believe it. But I should have known better. This is America, after all: where no effort is spared, no flight of fancy left unindulged, to cater to female histrionics.

There are antecedents for such behavior, if we look for them. Delusion is of old date. In 1597, the future King James I of England published a treatise, in the form of a Socratic dialogue, called *Daemonologie*. Although we chuckle today in smugness at James's credulity, witchcraft and sorcery were no laughing matter in the sixteenth century. Thousands of men and women were persecuted--many horrifically so-- for a "problem" that was entirely imaginary. James's book delves into the subjects of necromancy, ghosts, demons, and witchcraft with great enthusiasm, and makes his case that demonology not only exists, but also that *not believing* in these bugbears is itself a sin.

Has human nature advanced at all since 1597? Or have we only shifted our prejudices from witchcraft to other fantasies, like a "rape culture"? I wonder what our remote descendants will make of our delusions, and whether they will scratch their heads at our belief in imaginary rapes, just as we scratch our heads at James's devils, demons, and fairies. After all, James I was an intelligent and educated man. How could he allow himself to be sucked into such buncombe as belief in witchcraft and demons? The answer to this question lies in an understanding of human nature and the requirements of power. He was a king, and kings need to keep their thrones. Human nature needs fixations, in the same way that a dog needs to gnaw on bones; and systems of power and control thrive on creating and maintaining imaginary evils, so that their populations can be kept in a permanent state of turmoil. An uneasy population is a compliant one. Public service announcements in James's day were a bit different from what we see now, but the purpose was still the same: to whip up the public into a frenzy about a dubious problem, so that they become more open to suggestion. It is a tactic as old as government itself. Fear of marauding Parthians on the borders of the empire served this purpose during the age of the Antonines; nowadays, doctrinal deviations from political correctness function admirably as substitutes.

The alleged "problem" of endemic "rape" across the country is entirely imaginary. Authoritative studies have shown that crime of all types has been in steady decline for years. Yet, these apostles of doom continue to trumpet the approach of the non-consensual Apocalypse. One suspects that there are darker forces at work under the surface. It is often forgotten that such Cassandras serve a useful purpose for the forces that hold the reins of power in America: (1) they help to enforce cultural orthodoxy, and identify dissenting voices for persecution, and (2) they permit the power structure to solidify its hold on the mind of the population. America's rulers find it useful to deflect attention away from the real problems of society (vast income inequality, declining wages, masculinization of women, mediocre healthcare, education and services, etc.) onto imaginary problems. In such ways can the thefts carried out by the current American oligarchy be perpetuated at home and abroad.

I know a very sincere man who was infuriated by the public service announcement we saw at the movie theater. He asked how it was possible for men of obvious intelligence to believe such nonsense, and to permit themselves to make statements in the service of such stupidities. It is an important question, but a naïve one. These political figures and big actors in question don't really ask themselves whether they "believe" in rape culture or not, in the same way that a courtier of James I in 1600 would not have paused to reflect meaningfully on the "truth" of witches' Sabbaths. These are cynical, opportunistic people, who care only about their own positions.

It is not really a question that concerns them. What matters to them is power. Feminism is the dominant religion of the day, and they must—if they want to work—toe the party line. They know what they need to do in order to keep their salaries flowing, to get reelected, to keep their hold on their audience, and to maintain their thrones. That is as far as the thinking goes. On some subliminal level, of course, I think they convince themselves of the truth of their delusions. Reason can justify any weakness or vice. White knighting and mangina behavior is an expression of subservience to power. It is the ultimate form of degradation. And this is why I have more scorn and hostility to feminism's male supplicators than for feminism itself.

In Europe's religious wars of the sixteenth century, a principle emerged which summarizes the necessity of doctrinal orthodoxy among a ruler's subjects: *cuius regio, eius religio*. This

Latin phrase may be translated as: whose region, his religion. It was meant to convey the idea that the population under the control of a certain prince should accept that prince's religious doctrine, or else they should move elsewhere. In the modern era, princes find it useful to adhere to the same principle: subscribe to my doctrine, *or else*. In America, the prevailing religion is feminism, and the message conveyed the entirety of the culture is: you'd better toe the line, and believe in its demonology, or you are going to be persecuted. *Not to believe is itself a sin.*

There are other reasons, of course, for the propagation of the fake "rape culture." Some of these reasons have much to do with the idiosyncrasies of American society. Ours is a society steeped in fear: historically, fear of Indians, slaves, communism, terrorism, drugs, etc. Our society is a sexually repressive one, compared with most others; and for a repressed person, there is a perverse cruelty in denying sexual satisfaction to someone else. Most of the strident advocates of the "rape culture" are abnormal men and women. Miserable and repressed themselves, they wish to make everyone else just as miserable. There is also delight in being an accuser; it confers power and status, and is a form of attention-whoring.

So the requirements of power dovetail with the perversities and attention-whoring of "rape culture" advocates. It makes for a toxic mix. I remember reading a comment that Hermann Goering once made to one of his interviewers during his incarceration at the Nuremburg war crimes trials. The interviewer, a psychologist, asked him how he and his henchmen were able to seize and maintain control of the German government for so long. Goering chuckled and basically said, with his unique mix of brutal cynicism and charm, "It's easy, really. If you want to control people, all you have to do is make them believe they are under attack from someone or something. Then you can do whatever you want."

I think James I would have agreed with this, more or less.

21. How Our Enemies Confer Benefits On Us

A few days ago, a friend was talking to me about some injustice he had suffered from one of his enemies. He was furious at having been wronged. While I sympathized with him, some reflection on the matter cast the issue in a different light. It may even be stated, in the form of a general principle, that the vindictive actions of our enemies can serve as instruments for our continued upward growth. How this may be so, we will examine in this essay. It first must be appreciated that there can be no love without hate; no surfeit without want; and no real achievement without failure. The actions of our enemies make us appreciate the good things in life, and cause us to value more dearly the positive things of this world. Who can know love, without having experienced the sting of rejection? Who, never having gone hungry, can appreciate the satiety that comes from a full stomach? And who can appreciate the intoxication of victory, who has not felt the bitter sting of failure?

The actions of our enemies harden our sensibilities, and sharpen our cognitive faculties, so that we may be on our guard in life's inevitable struggles. The mountain goat conditions his stomach on rough fare, and grows strong on the bitterest and most miserable of food. Yet he who feasts only on delicacies gradually becomes effete and lacking in fortitude. The vulture, because he feeds on carrion, is counted by us as a disgusting and wretched animal; but for the ancient Romans, experienced in divination by auguries, he was a favored animal and a good omen. For a vulture never attacked a living man, and performed a useful function in removing a source of pestilence.

Our enemies teach us to be wary, and force us to watch our behavior. Your observations of your enemy will cause you to note his negative qualities: his meanness, cruelty, stupidity, and cowardice. Your increased awareness of these traits will help you to avoid them yourself; our enemies in this way become a form of external regulator. Only a fool will make no effort to learn from his enemies. And if we are honest with ourselves, even an enemy's criticism may hint at some secret deficiency on our part, and may cause us to redouble our corrective efforts at self-improvement. As the philosopher Diogenes noted, we often permit attacks on ourselves by our own improper conduct:

> To a young man who complained of the number of people who annoyed him by their attentions he said: 'Cease to hang out a sign of invitation.'[33]

Rare is it that some evil befalls us that we did not in some way allow to occur. Reflection on our contribution to our misfortunes will bring increased awareness of our own self-destructive conduct. Finally, it may also be that our enemy has positive virtues of his own, worthy of our own imitation. Give credit where it is due. To be blinded by hate is to miss an opportunity for reflection on how we may improve our own lot. When we are the target of abuse, our first impulse will be recklessly to respond in kind to the abuser; but calmer reflection may teach us to seek out what was the source of the criticism. By so identifying it, we may correct some flaw within ourselves. Even enemies have eyes, and may see us with more clarity than

---

[33] Diogenes Laertius VI.46. (trans. by R.D. Hicks; see note 22, *supra*).

friends. Our lovers, family, and friends will hesitate to be too honest with us. Affection clouds objectivity. Plutarch says, in his *Moralia*, quoting Antisthenes, that if we want to lead a good life, we ought to have either genuine friends or "red-hot enemies." Friends will deter us from what is wrong by admonition, enemies will deter us by ridicule.

An enemy's slanders also will cause us to take note how odious words of vituperation and calumny can be, so that we may avoid such mistakes ourselves. I remember when I began my career of arguing court cases. In those days, I would feel it necessary to respond to every insult, every slight, believing that such tit-for-tat tactics were necessary to get my point across. It was only later that I began to realize that allowing myself to descend into the mosh pit of mud-slinging accomplished very little, and detracted from the legitimate merits of my argument. Gradually, I learned to let my arguments speak for themselves. I avoided all intemperate speech and action in arguing my cases, and took care to let the effects of anger subside before responding to statements from the opposition. In this way, my results improved dramatically. Experience in dealing with hateful enemies also sharpens the edge of our courage, as confrontations become easier to bear with experience. A virgin blade is of dubious keenness.

We should be thankful for an enemy who attacks us openly, since a man brandishing a drawn dagger is easier to identify as an enemy than a man hiding a sheathed one. There is no opponent more dangerous than the one who lies in wait. As the number of bad characters we encounter in our lives is many, it is a good thing to be able to identify them as quickly as possible. Few enemies in our lives will pay us the compliment of revealing their hostility openly. They make our lives easier by declaring their intentions in advance. A quote that illustrates this point well is again by Diogenes, of whom it is said:

Being asked what creature's bite is the worst, [Diogenes] said, 'Of those that are wild, a sycophant's; of those that are tame, a flatterer.'[34]

Finally, an enemy can teach us the value of letting go of petty hostilities, and the redeeming virtue of forgiveness. Who may be an enemy one day, may become a friend on another. Few things are permanent in this world and, above all else, Fortune has a perverse sense of humor in making the unlikeliest of things possible.

---

[34] Diogenes Laertius VI.50. (See note 22, *supra*).

22. ON PILGRIMAGE

Travel writings, like travelers themselves, come in different forms. Some travel books offer a dull, tour-guide type of narrative, lacking serious reflection or insight. Other writings provide something deeper: an attempt to relate the impressions of the traveler in a way that transcends the physical act of travel. It is the latter type of writing that I value most. For it elevates travel from a task to a quest for knowledge and self-discovery. So the itinerant scholar Ciriaco de Pizzecolli (Cyriac of Ancona) rambled around the eastern Mediterranean in the 1440s, searching for and recording ancient inscriptions, manuscripts, and other antiquities, which he carefully recorded in his notebooks. And so also did humanist Biondo Flavio, traveling through Italy, seek to record the local folklore, geography, and historical oddities of the regions he visited. His masterpiece *Italia Illuminata*, appearing in1451, is a goldmine of strange information about Italy. Describing the Piceno region, for example, he relates this strange story:

Now except for recreational sex and adultery, which each of them enjoys in out-of-the-way places set up for this purpose, there is another crime committed in their public ceremonies. The more attractive women, whether widows, virgins, or wives, are called specifically and assembled in grottoes at night. Enclosed in the same cave…a cleric tells them in a loud voice that couples should…mingle in carnal sexual embrace. The lights are doused, and every man lays prostrate the woman next to him, either taking her or having observed her for this activity.[35]

Flavio reports some gruesome ritual murder practices of the cult, and ends by reassuring his readers that the members were eventually arrested and burned at the stake, "as indeed they deserved." Alas, not all travels are this exciting. Both Cyriac and Flavio were *pilgrims of the mind*, in a sense. They were on a quest for knowledge, and traveled with the specific purpose of learning something about their external world or themselves. Many people travel for work, and many for recreation. But how many travel specifically for the purpose of self-improvement or discovery? At one time, people did undertake travel for just such a purpose: it was called a pilgrimage. Whatever happened to the idea of the pilgrimage in the West? It has fallen out of fashion. And it is overdue for a resurrection. It can be an important vehicle to assist the modern man on his path to self-discovery and improvement.

Note that I do not necessarily mean a pilgrimage for religious purposes. By pilgrimage, I mean the act of travel to some "shrine" (house, building, tomb, etc.) of a great man, as a means of contemplating his life and what lessons it may hold. It is a sign of devotion, a method of meditation, a quest for guidance. Some background is in order here. Pilgrimages were a key part of medieval European religious devotion. The setting of Chaucer's *Canterbury Tales*, for example, was the pilgrimage of an assortment of characters. By the end of the thirteenth century, one historian tells us, there were about 10,000 sanctioned sites of pilgrimage all over Europe. People undertook such journeys to

---

[35] Flavio, Biondo, *Italy Illuminated* III.13. Text from White, J. (ed.), Cambridge: Harvard Univ. Press, 2005.

fulfill some vow, seek a cure by contemplating the relics of some saint or holy man, edify themselves, or for other personal reasons.

An Englishman, might, for example, visit the tombs of St. Cuthbert at Durham or Edward the Confessor at Westminster, or that of St. Edmund at Bury, or of Thomas a Becket at Canterbury. A Frenchman might seek out Notre Dame at Chatres, or St. Martin's at Tours. Italy, of course, had hundreds of such sites, among them the relics of St. Francis at Assisi or the Santa Casa at Loreto, as well as Rome itself. Sooner or later, all roads led to Rome, of course. Pope Boniface VIII declared a jubilee for the year 1300, and requested all who could to make the journey to Rome and visit the historical sites there. In that year over 2 million visitors reached Rome, a huge figure for those days. So many coins were deposited before the tomb of St. Peter that two priests working around the clock were needed to rake them in piles for collection. How did the idea of a formal pilgrimage as a method of self-improvement vanish? Few people today undertake such religious obligations, at least in the West. But could the idea of a pilgrimage still offer us something of value today? I believe it can. Instead of our focus being a religious site, we can instead seek out some site central to the life of a great man. By visiting the house, tomb, or architectural work of some great man, we will feel some sort of sympathy and kinship for his struggles. Such a visit will be a useful way of contemplating our own hardships, and how our historical "mentor" may have handled himself in similar circumstances.

Consider making a "pilgrimage" to some site intimately associated with a great man whom you admire. It does not matter who it is. It does not matter where it is. The only requirements are:

1. It must be to a site intimately associated with the great man in question (house, place of work, tomb).

2. The journey should not be too easy. You will value it more if you supply yourself with a bit of hardship.

3. You should visit the site, and contemplate the life of the great man in question while you are there. Then contemplate your own life. You should then record your impressions in writing. It will mean something to you someday.

There are thousands of such sites to choose from. It does not matter if your great man was a public figure, musician, leader, saint, artist, scholar, scientist, doctor, or poet. What matters is that you sincerely believe in his greatness, and the lessons that his life may hold as a candle to illuminate our own. The ecstasy of reaching a sought-after destination, after many trials and troubles, is one that has to be experienced to be fully appreciated. The journey, with all its hardships, is the major part of the reward of pilgrimage. We can begin to understand the joyous release of the medieval pilgrim, reaching the gates of Rome, singing the Pilgrims' Chorus:

O noble Rome, queen of the world...we bless you through all the years; through all the centuries, hail!

23. ASCENT INTO ETERNITY

On June 6, 1924, two haggard members of the British Everest Expedition, George Mallory and Andrew Irvine, left their frozen canvas tent on the wind-whipped side of Mount Everest and made a final push to reach the summit. It was the culmination of months of suffering, unrelenting effort, and danger, and the two men were confident that victory finally lay within their grasp. For Mallory, an experienced and tenacious alpinist, this was his last chance to achieve what had eluded him in previous summit attempts in 1921: to be the first man to reach the peak of the world's most formidable mountain. Having lost the race to be the first to the North and South Poles, British exploratory energy had invested much in Everest expeditions. But Mallory and Irvine never returned. On June 21, 1924, *The Times* of London published a telegraph from another team member announcing their death. It said only, "Mallory and Irvine killed on last attempt." The mystery of what had happened to them would continue to haunt Everest exploration ever since.

Fast forward to 1998. An American climbing enthusiast, Larry Johnson, emailed a twenty six year old German geology student and amateur climber named Jochen Hemmleb. Hemmleb had an encyclopedic knowledge of Everest expeditions. He had studied the subject intensely for many years and possessed an impressive archive of Everest arcana. He had published some of his writings on Everest exploration on a website for climbers, and had engaged in dialogue with other climbers in the website's forum section. Johnson and Hemmleb began a regular correspondence and eventually put together the idea of forming a commercial expedition to Everest for the purpose of investigating the fate of Mallory and Irvine. After countless false starts and frustrations, funding was secured, and team members were selected. The expedition moved forward in 1999. They called it the Mallory and Irvine Research Expedition.

As far as was possible, the plan was to retrace the steps of Mallory's ill-fated 1924 summit attempt. Over the decades, randomly discovered clues from climbers of different nationalities had suggested the presence of Mallory and Irvine in different places near the summit: a tent pole here, an ice axe there. But nothing was known with certainty. How had they perished? Where were they now? Beyond these questions lay the tantalizing possibility that the two men had actually reached the summit. If they had, the world would have to acknowledge that Sir Edmund Hillary, reaching the summit in 1953, was not the first.

Mallory had had a formidable reputation among mountaineers; thirty eight years old in 1924, he was generally recognized as one of the finest climbers of his day. Tall, resolute, a natural leader with restless energy, and possessed of a powerful physique, he was one of those urbane explorer-adventurers that England seemed to produce in abundance in the 19th and early 20th century. He was of an age where his strength of body was tempered by the practical prudence befitting his years. Readers should remember that this was an era before the high-tech comforts we take for granted: before Gore-Tex clothing, before labor-saving advanced mountaineering communications equipment, before synthetic materials, and before all the other comforts that modern explorers enjoy. Even bottled oxygen, that *sine qua non* of modern high-altitude mountaineering, was a novelty in 1924: Mallory himself only grudgingly accepted it after long debate.

Mallory and his men climbed Everest wearing woolen sweaters, leather boots, and clothing made from natural fibers. Looking at their "primitive" equipment now, with the knowledge of what climbers now take for granted, one is astonished at the toughness of these men. These were real men, not overgrown boys. And these were cultured men: in the frozen wastes of Everest, they would recite passages to each other from *King Lear* and *Macbeth* to pass the time and maintain morale. It was a different age. One can only grimace at the thought of what these men would make of our modern youth, with their marshmallow bodies, hover hands, neckbeards, and acquiescence to feminism. Take a good look at the faces in photos of these men. And take a good look at a photo of one of its members, Theodore H. Somervell. Somervell coughed up the lining of his throat during the summit attempt, and kept right on going.

The 1999 expedition had a general idea of how Mallory and Irvine had approached the summit, and were operating on the assumption that they might have fallen somewhere near the Northeast Ridge of Everest. Eventually the expedition members approached the Northeast Ridge, a perilous route from which some climbers over the years had plunged to their deaths. Team member Conrad Anker, acting on intuition, began to search on a low slope near the Rongbuk Glacier, traversing the rocky ground for signs of an ancient corpse. He eventually saw a bleached-white form lying on the rocky ground wearing a hobnailed boot, and moved forward to investigate. It was a corpse, it turned out, that had been holding fast to the side of Everest for seventy five years.

Most of the clothing had frayed away from the body, but the frozen white flesh had been preserved in Everest's unique environment. "The clothing was blasted from most of his body, and his skin was bleached white. I felt like I was viewing a Greek or Roman marble statute," said team member Dave Hahn. An examination of the name tag under the corpse's sweater revealed the name *G. Mallory*. The team members stood before the corpse in awe, hardly believing that they were viewing the remains of their fallen hero. What fortitude, what tenacity, in comparison to the over-equipped and pampered climbers of today! There was an inexpressible poignancy to the scene, a sense of kinship with those who had gone before them and participated in the great struggle to conquer the mountain.

With some effort, the team members searched the ground for artifacts and buried the body. The expedition had succeeded in discovering the fate of George Mallory, but the question of whether he or Irvine had actually reached the summit of Everest remained unanswered. No one really knows. Enthusiasts debate the issue with intensity, but it remains an unsettled question.

But what is beyond all dispute is the courage and tenacity of Mallory, Irvine, and the other members of the 1924 expedition. Laboring under conditions of extreme adversity, they set a high-water mark for Everest exploration that would not be matched for decades, until Sir Edmund Hillary achieved the first confirmed ascent of the summit in 1953. Actually reaching the summit has everything to do with raw guts and brute force, combined with favorable weather. The essence of masculine energy is breaking through barriers, overcoming obstacles, and achieving great things through unconquerable willpower and applied skill. To dream great things, to plan great enterprises, and to fight for their realization: are these not the secret flames that burn with unquenchable passion at the cores of our being? Look again at the fallen grandeur of George Mallory. Even in the repose of death, there is a supreme and silent dignity, a majesty, in this alabaster figure, preserved in startling whiteness and suspended in time, still grasping at the stony mountain which had claimed his life so long before. He lies there still, every inch a man. His fallen form chants its own regal poetry, to which we can add not a single verse.

24. CLASH OF STEEL AND WILLS:
THE STORY OF THE BATTLE OF LEPANTO

The climax of European military effort in the Mediterranean, and one of the most awe-inspiring naval engagements ever fought, was the Battle of Lepanto in 1571. A rickety, unlikely alliance of Christian states, cobbled together by Pope Pius V and held fast by the leadership of Don Juan of Austria, somehow managed to devastate the fleet, and humble the pride, of the invincible Ottoman Turks. The story has faded into obscurity. As an example of inspired leadership and tactical mastery, it has few equals. To place the battle in its proper perspective, we will first review the background.

Background

The Ottoman Empire in the 16th century was a superpower in every sense of the word. The fall of Constantinople in 1453 had sent shock waves through the Christian West that made thrones and popes tremble. But Western Europe, relatively weak and disorganized, could mount little effective resistance to the challenge from the East. The Turks rolled right through the Balkans and North Africa, and began to wrest control of eastern Mediterranean shipping from the Venice, which had long enjoyed a monopoly on maritime trade in the region. The Ottoman sultans had made no secret of their desire to bring all of Christian Europe under the banner of Islam; and to see their banner fly from the spires of the Vatican was not only hinted at, but was announced as inevitable. The Turks could back up such bellicose aspirations. Their military was powerful and organized: the feared Janissaries alone numbered over fifty thousand men, all of them disciplined professionals. To this number the sultans could draw on their vast empire for additional conscripts, slaves, and volunteers. By comparison, Europe after 1520 found itself ensnared in the turbulence and fratricide of the Protestant Reformation, too distracted and disunited to mount an effective resistance.

The eastern Mediterranean, especially the island of Cyprus, harbored many trading and naval outposts of Venice, which had been an integral part of her maritime and commercial power. But Venice was tired and in decline; her ports on the Ottoman doorstep were weak and undefended; and the Turks were confident and strong. The sultans' conclusions were obvious. In 1570 the Turks sent a force of over sixty thousand men to assault Cyprus. The Venetian colony of Nicosia fell in 1570 after a siege of forty five days; twenty thousand inhabitants were slain in the aftermath. Famagusta was attacked in 1571. The city resisted heroically for over a year, but in the end it surrendered after receiving assurances from the Turks that the defenders would be given safe passage home.

But the irate Turkish commander, Lala Mustafa, broke his word. He had the Venetian captives reduced to slavery or imprisonment. Marcantonio Bragadino, the city's head defender, was flayed alive in a gruesome act of revenge for the city's protracted resistance, which had cost the sultan about 50,000 men. Bragadino's preserved skin, stuffed with straw, was sent to Constantinople for the amusement of the sultan. Venice, roused to fury by this and other atrocities, sent frantic appeals to Pope Pius V and to the other powerful states of Europe for help.

The Diplomatic Situation

We should take note here of the posture and intentions of the major powers. Philip II of Spain led the most powerful state in Latin Christendom. He was engaged in his own intermittent wars against the Moslems of North Africa, who had appealed to the

Ottoman sultan for help. By general consent, the Spanish had the most disciplined, experienced, and best-led army in Europe. They were also zealous defenders of Catholicism, and their character—a passionate type, bearing much similarity to that of the Arabs, who had occupied Spain for six centuries and had stamped their imprint on the Spanish bloodline—was imbued with religious fervor and martial zeal. This was the era of Spanish glory and power. Having conquered the New World for the banner of Christ, and having expelled the last of the Moslem infidels from Spain in 1492, they had the ability and resources to confront the Turks.

The French and English, fearful of Spanish influence, were wary of participating in any enterprise that might enhance Spanish prestige. France even sought the friendship of the Ottoman sultan as an insurance policy against Spain. Even Venice, although she desperately needed aid, was fearful of bringing Spanish power into the eastern Mediterranean. The diplomatic abilities and deep pockets of Pope Pius V overcame all these difficulties, however, and managed to keep a delicate balance of trust between the allies. In 1571, he formed what came to be called the "Holy League", a coalition between Spain, the Papal States, Venice and Genoa, and the Knights of Malta.

The squabbling Italian city states were finally roused to unity to confront the Turkish threat. Aware that a Turkish fleet in 1566 had threatened the papal fortress of Ancona on the Adriatic Sea, a number of Italian principalities (Genoa, Savoy, Florence, Parma, Lucca, Ferrara, and Urbino) contributed to the effort of raising a fleet. The Spanish crown contributed the most men, money, and ships. A papal legate appointed Don Juan of Austria as commander at a ceremony in Naples. Capuchin monks and Jesuit priests were also attached to the expedition. It was a different age from our own. In those days, even clerics took up the sword, and fought and died alongside soldiers in battle, with an ardor befitting their station. Soldiers and sailors received the Eucharist on September 16, 1571, and the fleet sailed from Messina, heading for the island of Corfu in the Ionian Sea. The expedition was imbued with a passionate desire for revenge against the Turks for the deliberate cruelties that had accompanied the fall of Cyprus, and this militancy helped to overcome the national differences among the Holy League members.

As the Christian armada moved into the Gulf of Corinth, the Ottoman fleet was sighted, and Don Juan gave the order for his fleet to form in a battle line.

The Turkish commander had received orders from the sultan to engage the enemy, and so prepared his forces for combat. The composition of the belligerents was as follows: on the Turkish side, there were 222 galleys, 60 smaller ships, about 750 cannon, 34,000 soldiers, 13,000 sailors, and 41,000 oarsmen (almost all of them Christian slaves or convicts). On the Holy League side, there were 207 galleys, 6 Venetian galleasses (a Venetian invention which was a heavily-armed merchant galley converted for military use), 30 smaller ships, 1,800 cannon, 30,000 soldiers, 12,900 sailors, and 43,000 oarsmen. Besides their aggressive spirit, the Christian side possessed several advantages: (1) the Spanish infantrymen who composed the bulk of the Holy League forces were probably the best in Europe, and (2) the cannon and gunnery of Don Juan's fleet was superior to what the Turks could bring to bear.

The two massive fleets, one bearing the standard of the crucified Christ, and the other bearing the name of Allah embroidered in gold, made initial contact. All along the line of battle, shouts arose from the Holy League forces of *"Vittoria! Vittoria! Viva Christo!"* The left wing of the battle line, under the Venetians, advanced steadily, and the superior gunnery and ammunition of the Spanish and Italians made steady progress in reducing some of the sultan's ships to charred splinters. It was at this point that an act of singular courage and daring helped to tip the scales for a Christian victory.

Don Juan ordered his flagship to steer directly toward the Ottoman flagship, commanded by Muezzinzade Ali Pasha. His plan was to decapitate the Ottoman force by killing or capturing its leader. Naval combat in those days required opposing ships to throw out grappling hooks, and for one side to board the other, after which hand-to-hand combat would follow with cutlass, dagger, and pistol. And this is what happened when Don Juan's flagship collided in the blood-churned sea with the Turkish admiral's galleon.

Amid the smoke, confusion, and fury of battle, Don Juan gave the order to board Ali Pasha's vessel, named the *Sultana*. Three hundred Spanish veterans leapt aboard the enemy ship, their way led by a fearless Capuchin monk bearing nothing but a tunic and a crucifix; and the *Sultana's* deck ran red with blood and gore as the steel of battle-axes and cutlasses bit into the flesh of the combatants. Spanish pikemen raked the deck, cutting down the defenders in disciplined fury. The crash of metal upon metal reached a crescendo as the fighting see-sawed from one end of the ship to the other; and all around, as the galleons in the battle-line rolled and rocked, the screams of the fallen mixed with the acrid stench of gunpowder to add fear and confusion to the fight.

Ottoman Janissaries, the cream of the sultan's army, fought hand-to-hand with the Spanish *tercios*. The Spanish were repulsed several times, but kept coming back. It was an incredible sight, transcendent in its awesome carnage. This was the spirit that won the New World for Spain. Miguel de Cervantes (who would later achieve immortality for his authorship of the novel *Don Quixote*) was a participant in the battle, and was wounded during it. He later described it as "the most memorable occasion that either past or present ages have beheld, and which perhaps the future will never parallel."

The Ottoman flagship was overwhelmed by the Spaniards. Admiral Pasha Ali was slain and decapitated by a Spanish soldier, and his head suspended on his own flagstaff. At this sight, the morale of the Turks cracked, and their ships began to fall back under the steady pounding by Don Juan's gunners. When the smoke finally cleared hours later, over 10,000 Turks were taken prisoner and 8,000 slain; 117 ships were captured and 50 destroyed. On the Holy League side, 7,500 men were killed, 12 galleys were sunk, and about 12,000 Christian slaves (acting as Ottoman oarsmen) were freed. Countless corpses from both sides bobbed in the waves for miles. It was a devastating victory, a supreme achievement of Italian and Spanish arms, never to be equaled.

As with many decisive military victories, the victors were too exhausted or shocked to follow up their triumph with a pursuit of the enemy. It seems likely that, with the bulk of the Turkish fleet destroyed, a punitive expedition to Constantinople might have met with some success. But it was not to be. The victorious powers divided up the spoils of battle in proportion to their contribution to the expedition, and sailed home to universal acclaim in Europe.

In Venice and the rest of Catholic Europe, the celebrations were ecstatic. Church bells rang all over Europe. Men embraced each other in the street; artists immortalized the battle on canvas; and the Venetian doge was hailed as a hero. Rome was convulsed in joy, and Pius V nearly canonized Don Juan for his feats as admiral. He implored European leaders to assemble a military force for further attacks on the Ottomans, and tried to goad Persian and Arab leaders to launch their own strikes on the Turks. Nothing came of these efforts. Philip II of Spain was embroiled in his own struggles in the New World and in the Netherlands, France was secretly allied with the Turks in order to check Spanish power, and Venice had few friends outside of Italy. Pius V was praised and respected, but ignored. When he died in 1572, the concept of a second Holy League coalition was shelved.

Results

It can be argued that Lepanto changed little in the European equations of power. The Ottoman grand vizier, Mehmed Sokullu, remarked to a Venetian diplomat that Lepanto had done no permanent damage to Turkish power. Within six months after its defeat, the Ottoman Empire, showing great determination and skill, had rebuilt its fleet along Venetian models, incorporating lessons in tactics and gunnery learned at Lepanto. Venice continued to decline. The Ottomans raided Sicily and southern Italy soon after. By 1683 the Turks were in the heart of Europe, laying siege to Vienna.

But these facts ignore the central importance of Lepanto in destroying the myth of Ottoman invincibility. It was a psychological triumph of the first order. Once and for all, it was proven that the Turks did not have a monopoly on bravery and military skill. Although Turkish power continued to expand (of its own inertia) for a time after Lepanto, it is now clear that the battle provided a critical morale boost to harassed European Christendom. As the Europeans continued to innovate in military tactics, technology, and artistry, the Turks grew complacent and torpid. After 1580, the Ottoman fleet was allowed to deteriorate through neglect and ineptitude; from that point, the Ottomans were a decisive force on land only. Like other old Mediterranean powers, the Turks found themselves overtaken by the forces of history and geography. Most of these forces were beyond their control. With the discovery of the New World and its riches, everything changed; the Atlantic nations (Spain, England, Portugual, and The Netherlands) were positioned to dominate the new commercial global trade routes. The Mediterranean nations were forced to adjust themselves to the new alignments of economic power, and this meant a long period of decline and economic marginalization.

None of this detracts from the singularity of the Holy League's achievement at Lepanto. Few feats in naval history can compare with Don Juan's bold gamble in launching a direct assault on the Ottoman flagship and killing his rival commander. In war, as in the struggle of life itself, boldness and decision count for more than a hundred debates and discussions. This was an inspired move that took audacity and skill, and it was the turning point in the Battle of Lepanto.

Pre-battle plans and stratagems are always easy to come by. Every commander has a plan; every historian has an explanation; and every losing general has an excuse. But in war the plan usually goes out the window once the first shot is fired. In the end, discipline, brute strength, endurance, and tenacity matter more than delicate artistry. As the outcome of Lepanto hung in the balance, on the blood-stained deck of the *Sultana*, the Spanish infantry came face-to-face with the Janissaries. And the issue was decided by pike and cutlass.

25. THE LIMITS OF ENDURANCE

Pressure reveals the man. Take a man--any man--and subject him to extreme stress. Subject him to sleep deprivation or fear, exhaustion, and the uncertainties of climate and personal safety, and you will see the soul of the man. This is what I always liked about experiences of extreme stress. It reveals the true essence. A man's response can't be faked. It just can't. A young military trainee thrown into an extreme training environment or hostile fire zone, a young lawyer taking on his first jury trial, or a surgeon experiencing his first major operation on a patient, will all reveal their inner natures by their performances and responses to the duress of duty.

And sometimes we find out things about ourselves that we would rather not know. But it is a fascinating exposition. It is a wonder to behold. Those who enter these dark arenas are driven by a desire to test their cold steel against the flesh of the world. It is truly the greatest drama of all. And you never can tell. You never can. That man you see over there, for instance, who seems to be a quiet, bespectacled introvert, may turn out to have the soul of a lion. Or that peacocking, muscled braggart over there may be revealed to be a man of straw at the moment of truth. Or vice-versa. You just never can be certain. But every man has a breaking point. I remember reading a story in Tom Mangold and John Penycate's book *The Tunnels of Cu Chi*[36] some years ago that

---

[36] New York: Berkley Publishing Group, 1986.

resonated with me and stuck in my memory. I want to relate it here.

Jack Flowers was a college dropout who got drafted into the US Army the late 1960s and found himself serving in Vietnam. Because of his educational background, he was put through an officer training program and was assigned to an engineer battalion. Over time, he began to feel the stirrings of an unsuspected militancy, and became more and more interested in taking an active part in the fighting. Two experiences helped push him in this direction. One was getting called a REMF (rear echelon motherfucker), and another was seeing a dead comrade getting pulled out of a Viet Cong tunnel.

Like some men, he was driven by an inner, secret pride that felt compelled to test the limits of its endurance. Flowers would soon get his chance. Against the advice of his friends and family he decided to join an elite group of "tunnel rats", which specialized in locating and destroying the enemy in its dark honeycomb of underground lairs. Armed only with a switchblade, flashlight, revolver, and maybe a grenade, a tunnel rat had to go down into the tunnels, seek out the enemy, and kill him in one-on-one combat.

By all accounts, combat in the tunnels was a horrifying experience. It was as personal as the war ever got. And there was no way to fake it. The man who had trained and led the tunnel rats which Flowers joined was a smoldering, inscrutable soldier named Sergeant Robert Batten. He was nicknamed Batman. And he was both widely feared and respected for his extraordinary body counts and ruthless leadership abilities. Batten was a legend, and he knew it. He was a tough, cunning, and deeply aggressive man; someone who might have been a nonentity in regular life but had come into his own during the war. The Viet Cong knew who he was, and had put him on their "ten most wanted" list. Captured VC spoke of him with awe. Batten didn't like most officers, and he didn't like poseurs. Incompetents and fake heroics could get men killed. Everyone had to pull his weight; there was no rank in the tunnels. "We'll get along just fine if you stay out of my way" was his curt statement to Flowers. The tunnel rats were a highly professional unit. There were many Puerto Ricans and Mexicans, men coming from cultures for whom the martial spirit of Old Spain had never really died, men who were not squeamish about using a knife, men who had never gotten much from life and expected little from it. There were also many quiet, unassuming hillbilly types, men who were otherwise soft-spoken but who became unglued in the tunnels, relishing in the subterranean duels.

Man is a complex and many-layered being. Slowly and steadily, Flowers built up his credibility with Batten and the tunnel rats, and earned their respect. He knew he could never ask one of his men to do something he himself would not do, so he personally went on many tunnel missions. He began to lead his unit in fact as well as in theory. He was even wounded by a grenade on a tunnel mission with Batten. And his confidence soared. He was a good "Six" (tunnel rats used the term "Six" as the code word for leader). He had wanted to prove to Batten that he was his equal, that he was a good fighter, and a good leader.

Batman was unimpressed. He had sized up Flowers in his own way, and issued his own verdict. One day, Batten said to him, "You're not a killer, Six, and that's your problem. You're pretty good, the best Six I ever had, but you'll fuck up somewhere. Charlie hasn't killed a rat for quite a time. And you'll either let him get you, or you'll get yourself." Flowers was stung by the remark, but let it go. Batten rotated out of Vietnam soon after, having served three back-to-back tours.

One day, Flowers and his men were out on a mission. A tunnel complex was discovered and someone spotted a VC disappear down a shaft that went straight down twenty feet before angling off horizontally. They thought they had the VC cornered. He had to be down there, crouching in the horizontal tunnel with his AK-47 ready. Flowers was exhausted but pressed on. He looked down the shaft, a rat hole leading straight to hell. He decided to have his men lower him in a seated rope cradle (called a Swiss seat) halfway down the shaft. They would then drop him, and he would hit the bottom of the shaft so he could take the cornered VC by surprise. One of the rules of the tunnel rats was never to fire more than three shots from a .38 revolver, as this would reveal that the shooter needed to reload. As Flowers was lowered slowly down into the shaft, his men looked on in grim silence. He was soaked in sweat, throbbing with adrenaline, and he kept hearing Batten's voice, over and over again, a broken phonograph record whose grooves played the same sentence.

You'll fuck up somewhere, Six...you'll either let him get you, or you'll get yourself.

His plan was to hit the ground and immediately get off a head shot against the VC before he himself was hit. He fully expected to get hit, and, as he was lowered slowly into the hole, he tried to visualize the best shooting position to get into. The sweat was pouring off him and began to fall in steady drops on the tunnel floor. Finally Flowers gave the signal and he was dropped into the inky blackness. He hit the ground and started firing. And kept firing. After his men heard six shots ring out, one of them threw down a second revolver. And then there was silence. When the smoke of cordite cleared, Flowers breathlessly tried to make out what was in front of him. Nothing but a blank dirt wall. No VC with a gun. Just a cluster of bullet holes in the earth. Exhausted and stressed beyond limit, he had fired all six rounds against an imaginary target. And the rules said no more than three shots. Flowers rubbed his fingers against the six neat holes in the packed earth wall, and then put his head in his hands. And in his mind, he heard Batten's taunting voice.

You'll get yourself, Six. You'll get yourself...

Word of the incident found its way back to Flowers's commanding officer, and he was relieved. Not much was said, but it was clear that his men had lost confidence in him. For the good of the unit, he was shipped out of the area to another part of Vietnam. There were no goodbyes, no pats on the back, nothing. He was just gone. And then Flowers secluded himself and stayed drunk for a week. He had found his limits, and his war was over. He had done his job with honor, and tested the hazy boundaries of his own endurance and tenacity. He had nothing to be ashamed of.

The Greek philosopher Heracleitus believed above all else in the ubiquity, and transcendent power, of Fire and Change. Fire was the soul of the world, the eternal principle that underlay all that is or was in the cosmos. Even man himself was a form of Fire: with each passing moment, part of us dies while another part lives. These points of death and life, he believed, are arbitrarily drawn chalk marks in the continuum of eternity. The only constant is change. The great struggles of life leave no one unscathed. No one is exempt; there is no opting out of this Eternal Principle. And as character determines fate, there is no escape from the pitiless confrontation between man and his individual destiny. It makes us, and it breaks us. The obscenities of armed conflict strip us down, flay the protective layers of delusion from our bodies, and expose us to the twin indignities of violence and truth. No other tribunal is more unyielding, or more merciless.

26. A MAN UNIQUE: ERNST JÜNGER'S FIRE AND FURY

An expert in classical Chinese once wrote that ancient texts occasionally feature characters that appear once, and only once, in the existing literature. The linguistic term for such words or characters is *hapax legomenon*. Because of this uniqueness, we are told, it is not possible to know precisely the meaning of a *hapax* character. A scholar, for example, might be confronted by a sentence that reads, "The chariot moved across the battlefield with the furious speed of an X." One translator, using his best informed guess, might render X as meaning such-and-such; and another translator might render X as something else. But the truth is that we can never know precisely what the meaning of the character X is. It is unique. There are no other textual contexts in which we may evaluate it. As a *hapax legomenon*, it will remain forever cloaked in mystery.

Men can also be *hapax* figures. They disturb the convenience of our lazy taxonomies by refusing to be pidgeon-holed as one thing or another. Such men defy easy categorization; they can never precisely be pinned down to our butterfly-board. Just such a contradictory character was German writer Ernst Jünger. Impassioned warrior, biologist, writer, philosopher, mystic, nationalist, and believer in psychedelic drugs, Jünger stands nearly alone among twentieth century writers, laughing at our attempts to fit him into any one box. He was born in Heidelberg in 1895 and had a reasonably comfortable middle-class upbringing. Running away from home in 1913 to join the French

Foreign Legion, he served briefly in North Africa, after which his father brought him home.

Still lusting for combat, he volunteered for the Kaiser's army in 1914 and served with great distinction on the western front as an infantry officer and storm trooper. He received the Iron Cross First Class in 1917, and finally Imperial Germany's highest military decoration, the fabled "Blue Max" (the *Pour le Merite*) at the age of 23 in 1918. Wounded many times during night patrols and trench raids, Jünger found the war to be a supremely transcendent experience, a distillation of the struggle of life, and the core of masculine identity. Throughout the war, Jünger kept a private diary of his experiences, and these scattered thoughts formed the nucleus of a book which he self-published in 1920 under the title *In Stahlgewittern*. Appearing in English under the martial title *Storm of Steel*, the memoir catapulted Jünger to prominence. There is nothing like it in all war literature. It deserves close examination on our part. As a hospital orderly once told Jünger philosophically while dressing one of his wounds: *habent sua fata libelli et balli* ("books and bullets have their own destinies.")

The first thing that strikes us in *Storm of Steel* is the tone: here there is no morose hand-wringing as one might find in the weepy writings of Erich Maria Remarque, Siegfried Sassoon, or Robert Graves; none of the clinical detachment of Adolf Von Schell's lifeless *Battle Leadership*; and none of the pacifist sniveling that mars some of the work of Ernest Hemingway. Instead, we are thrown right into the thick of the action, swept up with Jünger in the exhilaration of proximity to instant death, as bombs burst all around us and a determined enemy is waiting beyond the lip of our trench to cut our throats. The Greek philosopher Heracleitus believed that Fire was the essential force that moved the world; and under the spell of Jünger's prose, we actually come to believe this to be so. We are stupefied by the lyric poetry of flame, fist, and iron, as the earth trembles beneath our feet during artillery

150

bombardments; and we huddle with Jünger in soggy, putrid shell holes, waiting for the opportunity to plunge a dagger into a British Tommy's gut.

Jünger takes it all in with the wry humor and determination of a true combat soldier, never boring us with mealy-mouthed questions about the war's origins and purpose. For him, the war is a mystical experience, bringing an elevated awareness of the agonies and joys of life. Combat and pain are the quintessence of life. There is only survival in the present moment, and the supreme experience of hunting down and killing the enemy. Among countless memorable passages, the following will give a flavor of the whole:

The trench was appalling, choked with seriously wounded and dying men. A figure stripped to the waist, with ripped-open back, leaned against the parapet. Another, with a triangular flap hanging off the back of his skull, emitted short, high-pitched screams. This was the home of the great god Pain, and for the first time I looked through a devilish chink into the depths of his realm. And the fresh shells came down all the time.[37]

Jünger's prose approaches poetry with this sentence, describing the German response to an attack by French aircraft:

The anti-aircraft guns threaded long fleecy lines through the air, and whistling splinters pinged into the tilth.[38]

---

[37] Jünger, Ernst, *Storm of Steel*. New York: The Penguin Group, 2003, p. 31.
[38] Id., p. 35.

About the thrill of marauding by night into enemy lines, Jünger has this to say:

These moments of nocturnal prowling leave an indelible impression. Eyes and ears are tensed to the maximum, the rustling approach of strange feet in the tall grass is an unutterably menacing thing. Your breath comes in shallow bursts; you have to force yourself to stifle any panting or wheezing. There is a little mechanical click as the safety-catch of your pistol is taken off; the sound cuts straight through your nerves. Your teeth are grinding on the fuse-pin of the hand-grenade. The encounter will be short and murderous. You tremble with two contradictory impulses: the heightened awareness of the huntsman, and the terror of the quarry. You are a world to yourself, saturated with the appalling aura of the savage landscape.[39]

Describing the ghastly contradictions of combat, he notes ironically:

We started to dig trenches right across the village, and erected new walls near the most dangerous places. In the neglected gardens, the berries were ripe, and tasted all the sweeter because of the bullets flying around us as we ate them.[40]

And here, Jünger dispatches an enemy soldier with emotionless precision:

---

[39] Id., p. 71.
[40] Id., p. 89.

I spotted a British soldier breaking cover behind the third enemy line, the khaki uniform clearly visible against the sky. I grabbed the nearest sentry's rifle, set the sights to six hundred, aimed quickly, just in front of the man's head, and fired. He took another three steps, then collapsed onto his back, as though his legs had been taken away from him, flapped his arms once or twice, and then rolled into a shell-crater, where though the binoculars we could see his brown sleeves shining for a long time yet.[41]

After the war, Jünger remade himself as a biologist and entomologist, although insects were never quite as appealing as combat. By his own admission, he "hated democracy" and parliamentarianism, and was a conservative nationalist. Yet to his credit, he also despised fascism and National Socialism. He refused a seat in Hitler's Reichstag in 1933, forbade his writings to appear in Nazi publications, and was careful to distance himself from any endorsement of Hitler. He was mobilized for military service in the Second World War, but spent the war years mostly in occupation duty in Paris. Jünger remained a committed individualist, never wanting to be beholden to anyone. After 1945, he was briefly banned from publishing for his refusal to kow-tow to the Allied occupation authorities. He continued to write, however, eventually turning out more than fifty titles. In the postwar years, his uniqueness shone forth in all its intensity.

In his treatise *On Pain*, he argued that the experience of pain, and man's capacity to deal with it, was the central question of the human condition in the modern era. More bizarre was his enthusiasm for hallucinatory drugs: his later writings (e.g.,

---

[41] Id., p. 126.

Approaches, appearing in 1970) chronicle his dalliances with cocaine, hashish, and LSD. He was also an adherent of the "magical realism" movement, a literary school which held that magical or fantastic qualities permeate the experience of ordinary life. We cannot be sure he was wrong. Actually, Jünger led a charmed life, outlasting nearly everyone. Gradually his literary star rose to prominence; by the 1960s and 1970s, he was one of Germany's most respected writers. In 1984, he, along with the presidents of France and Germany, he dedicated a battlefield memorial at Verdun and publicly condemned militarism.

He never regretted or apologized for anything he wrote, proudly proclaiming his belief in the power of the individual over that of the mechanized state. He died in 1998 at the age of 102. German Idealism, which had begun with Fichte, Schelling, and Hegel, had seemed almost a spent force until the advent of *Storm of Steel*. In many ways, he was the final, explosive culmination of the stubborn Idealist strain in German thought, a thread that thankfully has not quite yet died out. But Jünger is stranger still; his body of work synthesizes so many disparate strands that he really is in a class by himself. As a lyric poet of total war, and as an apostle of the cathartic power of combat, he remains unsurpassed. He is a Teutonic *hapax legomenon*, a character standing alone, whose true meaning we can only guess at.

27. THE LIVES OF GREAT MEN
AS MORAL INSTRUCTION

There is no better school of instruction for our own lives than in learning about the lives and trials of great men. By following their experiences, struggles, and adversities, we can in some way calibrate our own responses to life's inevitable whirlwinds. The reward is made even greater when the narrator of such biographies is an urbane, classically-trained rhetorician whose primary focus is on the moral development of his readers. Just such a teacher is Plutarch. Plutarch (c. A.D. 45-- c. 120) was a Greek writer who received the best education possible in his day; he served in several official posts, and received official recognition from the Roman emperors Trajan and Hadrian for his writings.

Plutarch is primarily famous for his *Parallel Lives*, which is a compendium of comparative biographies of famous Greek and Roman statesmen. His other major work, the *Moralia*, is a collection of essays, dialogues, and observations on various moral and philosophical subjects. Both of these works make for wonderful reading, but I want to focus on the *Parallel Lives* here, as it is more likely to be of interest to the average reader. There is no other work quite like Plutarch's *Parallel Lives*. He must have had to collate and synthesize dozens of original sources, much of it in a language that was not native to him. Some of what we know about major figures of antiquity appears in no other work than in his.

Plutarch's main motivation was to examine what factors made great men great, and how the average man could employ those virtues. He pairs an eminent Greek with an eminent Roman (choosing figures with lives that roughly had some things in common, such as Theseus and Romulus, Lycurgus and Numa Pompilia, Solon and Publicola, etc.), and outlines the life of each figure. Then, in a conclusory essay, he compares both figures and tells us the key virtues of each, and why he believes one was better than the other. This comparative technique suits his purposes admirably: it brings into sharp focus the qualities, decisions, and actions that made each great man great. Another virtue of the *Parallel Lives* is the quality of the writing. There is here no turgid prose, no boring digressions. Every sentence counts, every paragraph sparkles with anecdotes, explanations, and an epigram that drives home the author's point. This is history presented as a moral exercise.

We can judge the quality of the *Parallel Lives* by their unbroken popularity down the centuries. They were cherished by Renaissance humanists, plundered for plots by Shakespeare, pored over hungrily by Montaigne, and beloved by Napoleon. Scarcely has any one book so instructed statesmen over such a long period. The most important quality of the *Lives*—what gives it its charm–is that Plutarch is writing as a teacher of men. He is mindful of our development and sincerely wants to be our guide. In his day, the education of young men was concerned as much with the development of character and morals as with the imparting of knowledge. (This focus, of course, is sorely missed today). Modern biographies do not normally provide this sort of thing: they are more concerned with cluttering their narratives with footnotes and scholarly apparatus than with helping us become better men.

There are many versions of the *Lives* in print, and choosing which one can present something of a problem and a compromise. Plutarch's original plan was to have the reader work through each pairing together, and then read his comparison essay at the end. Unfortunately, the *Lives* stretch through several thick volumes, and many readers will not want to wade through them all. Buying the entire set is not practical for most (although recommended). Some readers will only want to read about Greeks, some only about Romans.

Editors over the years have often chopped up the *Lives* in various ways, which does violence to Plutarch's literary plan and pedagogical purpose. From examining several editions of the *Lives*, my opinion is that retaining some of Plutarch's comparative pairing scheme is vital. I like the Penguin editions the best: the editors group the biographies into periods of time and by nation, but still keep the best comparative essays.

I want to close this article by saying a few related words. Now, more than ever, young men are in critical need for instruction and self-improvement. Never before have so many been so lost, and so in need of guidance. The quest to enrich, ennoble, and improve ourselves has become, to use the words of H.G. Wells, "a race between education and catastrophe." Readers will note that I have long emphasized historical and philosophical topics as ways to make larger points. There is a deliberate reason for this. By invoking the past, I have tried to remind readers of the glories of leadership, character, and masculine virtue that can change their lives. By bringing up the past, a time before masculine virtues were shamed and punished, we remind readers of the glories that will be theirs if they follow the right paths. "The mind is not a vessel to be filled," says Plutarch, "but a fire to be kindled."

Sadly, there are forces which do not want to see us improve: these forces seek to emasculate us, to turn us into compliant hewers of wood and drawers of water for ideologically driven overlords. One can even imagine a future where classical knowledge will be driven underground, purged from schools, or bowdlerized, as not being in tune with modern feminism and political correctness. The degradation of humanistic learning has come as a direct result of the feminization of American society. We cannot permit this to happen. The commissars of modern culture don't want you to know too much about history, or about how things were like in previous eras.

This would invite uncomfortable questions, and comparisons with the sorry state of masculinity today. But we go about our work regardless. We know our readers better than they. We have lived their same struggles, hungers, and secret aspirations, and have always viewed the inner longings of our brothers with patience and understanding. We know that many of our readers, in this era, are being allowed to flounder helplessly in a wilderness not of their own choosing, with their masculine potential denigrated or scorned by a media elite that values only feminist frivolities and dialectic. This tide will be reversed. And we will forever remain passionately dedicated to restoring the lost glory that once was ours.

28. MACHIAVELLI'S COMIC SIDE

Everyone knows Niccolo Machiavelli's (1469-1527) status as a seminal political theorist, but few are also aware that he was also a first-rate playwright and satirist. His play *Mandragola* (probably written around 1519) is one of the outstanding comedies of the Italian Renaissance stage. You've likely never even heard of it. Of course, once you learn the plot, you'll get a pretty good idea why you're not likely to see this play staged by your local community college theatre group anytime soon. Modern commissars of political correctness dare not allow it. Machiavelli opens the play with a brief prologue in which he warns off any anticipated critics:

Should anyone seek to cow the author by evil-speaking, I warn you that he, too, knows how to speak evil, and indeed excels in the art; and that he has no respect for anyone in Italy, though he bows and scrapes to those better dressed than himself.

This was no idle threat. Invective and calumny were common pastimes among the literati in Italy then (as now), and few could sling mud as well as Machiavelli. The play is set in Florence. Callimaco, our sensual protagonist, prides himself on his skills with women. He hears someone praise the great beauty of Lucrezia, the wife of Nicias. Although Callimaco has never seen her, he at once decides that he must seduce her, if only so he can sleep peacefully. However, Lucrezia is also known for her virtue, and this may be an obstacle. Callimaco sees an opening when he learns that Nicias is depressed over Lucrezia's failure to conceive a child. Callimaco bribes a friend to introduce him to Nicias as a doctor. Callimaco tells Nicias that he has a special "medicine" that can make any woman fertile; but the only problem, says Callimaco, is that the first man who sleeps with a woman taking the special potion may die.

Callimaco generously offers to "risk his life" to sleep with Lucrezia, and the gullible beta-male Nicias eventually agrees. Lucrezia, however, remains modest and is not keen on the plan. Fortunately for Callimaco, Lucrezia's mother is especially desirous of grandchildren. So the mother bribes a priest for twenty five ducats to advise Lucrezia, in the confessional, to agree to the plan. The bribed priest convinces her. She drinks the potion, sleeps with Callimaco, and becomes pregnant. Basically, everyone is happy at the end; everyone gets what they wanted. Callimaco can rest at ease, knowing he has slept with the Lucrezia; Nicias has a child; and the priest can count his money while reciting benedictions.

All in all, the play is a brilliant comedy. It is also amazing to learn that it was performed successfully in 1520 before Pope Leo X in Rome. The fact that the play celebrated sex and seduction, and ridiculed the clergy as frauds, bothered him not at all. In fact, the Pope liked it so much that he asked Cardinal Giulio de Medici to award Machiavelli a commission as a writer. What can we conclude from all this? What is surprising—even shocking—for modern audiences is the theme that fraud and deception are actually good things. Not only is fraud not punished, but it is actually presented as a virtue, as long as everything turns out all right in the end. It is refreshing to hear someone celebrate the unapologetic pursuit of sensualism.

The biographers tell us that in his personal life, Machiavelli fully enjoyed the pursuits of the flesh. When close to fifty years of age, he wrote to a friend, "Cupid's nets still enthrall me. Bad roads cannot exhaust my patience, nor dark nights daunt my courage…My whole mind is bent on love, for which I give Venus thanks." He also sent detailed letters of his sexual adventures to his friends, some of which are so frank that publishers to this day hesitate to print them. If *Mandragola* were made into a film today, we can just imagine how it would be watered down. Feminism and political correctness would neuter its satiric impact, its pungent sexuality, and its salty ribaldry. It would probably be turned into an ode to girl-power, with the standard Hollywood metrosexual beta male in the role of Callimaco, and the other men reduced to simpering lackeys. Picture a dour and snarky Jennifer Aniston as Lucrezia, lecturing the audience in dreary monologues on the evils of male sexuality. Imagine Seth Rogen in the role of Callimaco, now safely beta-ized; and visualize Jack Black in a standard gibberish-spewing appearance as Nicias.

Powerfully written, and a brilliant satire. Just don't expect to see it staged anytime soon.

29. EIGHT FILMS

When I ask myself what films in recent years have been my favorites, I find that the answers all seem to have a few things in common. One, the movie must tell a compelling story; two, it must rise above its genre to make a larger statement about life or some universal idea; and three, it must be technically well made. All great art—including film—can serve as a vehicle for the presentation of ideas, and the promotion of a certain virtue. Although the mainstream American film industry has become more and more a sad repository of feminist cant and lowest-common-denominator commercial pandering, the foreign film world has undergone something of a renaissance in the past fifteen years.

The best films of France, Germany, Spain, and the UK are edgier, more intelligent, and more masculine than much of what we find in America. It was not always so. But the work of great European directors like Jacques Audiard, Gaspar Nöe, Nicolas Winding Refn, and Shane Meadows leaves little room for doubt that the true cutting-edge work is being done in Europe. (Argentina deserves honorable mention here as having an excellent film industry). The mainstream, corporate-driven US film industry has effectively smothered independent voices under an avalanche of political correctness, girl-power horseshit, and mind-numbing CGI escapist dreck.

Movies that deal with masculine themes in a compelling way are not easy to come by these days. Honest explorations of masculine virtues are repressed, marginalized, or trivialized. One needs to scour the globe to cherry-pick the best here and there, and in some cases you have to go back decades in time. Luckily, the availability of Netflix and other subscription services has made this task much easier than it used to be. Access to the best cinema of Europe, South America, and Asia can be a great way for us to catch a glimpse at a foreign culture, as well as reflect on serious ideas.

I want to offer my recommendations on some films that I believe are an important part of the modern masculine experience, in all its wide variety and expression. Out of the scores of possible choices, I decided to pick the handful of films that are perhaps not as well known to readers. My opinions will not be shared by all. I encourage readers to draw up their own lists of films dealing with masculine themes, and hope they will reflect on the reasons behind their choices. Below are mine, in no particular order. In italics is a brief plot synopsis, followed by my own comments.

1. Straw Dogs (1971)

A mild-mannered American academic (Dustin Hoffman) living in rural Cornwall with his beautiful wife becomes the target of harassment by the local toughs. Things escalate to a sexual assault on his wife, and eventually to a brutal and protracted fight to the death when a local man takes refuge on their property.

This is a classic example of the type of movie that could never be made today. Arguably Sam Peckinpah's most daring film, it contains a controversial rape scene that seems to leave open the question whether Hoffman's wife (played by Susan George) was a victim or a willing participant. Faced with his wife's betrayal, and continuing harassment from local rogues, Hoffman's character finds himself completely isolated and must learn to stand his ground and fight. A chance incident later in the film sets the stage for a blood-soaked confrontation which is as inevitable as it is necessary. Peckinpah presents a compelling case for the cathartic power of violence, and the achievement of masculine

163

identity through man-on-man combat. It is a theme I find myself strongly drawn to. Peckinpah proves himself an unapologetic and strident advocate of old-school martial virtue. We would do well to listen. His voice is sorely missed today. (Note: avoid the pathetic recent remake of this movie). Honorable mention in the Peckinpah canon here includes *The Wild Bunch* (1969) and *Bring Head of Alfredo Garcia* (1974).

2. Sorcerer (1977)

A group of international renegades find themselves down and out in Nicaragua, and volunteer for a job transporting unstable dynamite across the country to quell an oil rig fire.

Due to inept marketing when this movie was first released, it never achieved the credit it so fully deserved. A motley group of international riff-raff (including the always appealing Roy Scheider) seeks redemption through a harrowing trial. But will they get it? Is it even desirable to escape one's dark past? The answers are complex, and director William Friedkin refuses to supply easy ones. The characters in this film are doomed, and they know it, but they still hold true to their own code. Which is itself honorable. Consequences must be paid for everything we do in life, and often the price comes in a way never expect. Dark, brooding, and humming with a pulse-pounding electronic score by Tangerine Dream, this film has deservedly become a cult classic. The ending is a shocker you'll never see coming.

3. The Lives of Others (2006)

A coldly efficient Stasi (East German security service) officer (Ulrich Mühe) is enlisted by a Communist party hack in a surveillance program against a supposed subversive writer and his girlfriend. But monitoring the writer's life awakens sparks of nascent humanity in the Stasi man, and he eventually must decide whether to follow orders and destroy the writer, or to sacrifice himself to save him.

This German masterpiece was made with great fidelity to the look and feel of 1980s East Germany, and the results are evident in every frame. It belongs on any list of the greatest films ever made. The masculine virtue here is of a different type than viewers may be used to: it is a quiet, understated heroism, the type of heroism that probably happens every day but is hardly noticed. There is no bragging here, no chest-beating, no big-mouthed bravado. (In short, none of the wooden-headed caricatures that pass for masculinity in the US). The ethic here is about love and self-sacrifice, the noblest and greatest virtues of all.

The ethos of self-sacrifice is now considered old-fashioned and almost a punch-line, but historically it was valued highly. It features in nearly all the old literary epics and dramas of Europe and Asia. Actor Ulrich Mühe pulls off a minor miracle of characterization here with his portrayal of a Stasi man named Weisler, whose special wiretapping assignment against a playwright transforms him from heartless automaton into awe-inspiring hero. The movie made me wonder just how many quiet, unassuming men there must be out there, whose quiet toil and sacrifice has never been, and never will be, acknowledged. The ending is transcendent, and moving beyond words.

4. Homicide (1991)

A police detective (Joe Mantegna) is assigned to investigate a murder case. The case awakens in him stirrings of his long-suppressed ethnic identity. Unfortunately, he will eventually be forced to choose between conflicting loyalties. And the consequences will be devastating.

No modern American director has probed the meaning of masculine identity more than David Mamet, and all of his films

165

are meditations on themes related to illusion, reality, masculinity, and struggle. *Homicide*, a nearly unknown gem from the early 1990s, is perhaps his profoundest. Mamet knows that a man must make choices in his life, and for those choices, consequences must be paid. And very often, we find ourselves derailed by the mental edifices we construct for ourselves. The Mantegna character is led through a complex and increasingly ambiguous chain of events, only to find that at the heart of one mystery lies an even more inscrutable one. Mamet's message is this: beware the things you seek. You may not like what you find.

5. A Prophet (2009)

An Algerian Arab is incarcerated in a French jail, and is drawn into the savage world of Corsican gangsters. Forced to kill or be killed, he is drawn into a pitiless world that recognizes only cunning and brutality. He finds himself straddling two realities: the world of his own nationality, and that of the Corsicans. And to survive and emerge triumphant, he must learn to play all sides against each other.

This film must be counted among the greatest crime dramas ever made. You simply can't take your eyes off the screen. The lesson here is that a man must learn to survive on his wits, and do whatever is necessary to stay alive. The Corsican boss whom Al Djebena (Tahar Rahim) works for is just about the most malevolent presence in recent screen memory. Part of France's continuing internal dialogue about its immigrant population, *A Prophet* is not to be missed.

6. The Beat That My Heart Skipped (2005)

An intense young man (Romain Duris) works for his father as a real estate scammer in urban Paris. His "job" consists of intimidating deadbeat immigrant tenants, vandalizing apartments, and forcibly collecting loans. He also plays the

166

piano. Eventually, he is forced to decide which life he wants: the path laid out by his shady father, or the idealistic path of his own choosing. He's seeking redemption, but will he find it? And at what cost?

Again, we have here the themes of redemption and moral choice. Romain Duris has a screen presence and intensity that rivals anything done by Pacino in his prime, and some of the scenes here are fantastic. (His seduction of his friend's wife, Aure Atika, is one of many great scenes). All men will be confronted and tested by crises and situations beyond their control. How they respond to those situations will define who they are as men. Duris's character proves that redemption can be achieved, if wanted badly enough.

7. Red Belt (2008)
Martial arts instructor Mike Terry is forced, against his principles, to consider entering a prize bout. He is abandoned and betrayed by his wife and friends, and must confront his challenges alone with only his code and his pride.

Another great meditation on masculine virtue and individualism by David Mamet. In his own unique dialogue style, Mamet showcases his belief that, in the end, all men stand alone. At the moment of truth, it is you, and only you, who will be staring into the abyss. Our trials by fire will not come in the time and at the place of our own choosing. They may even come, as in the movie, in a bare passageway leading to an arena. But when they do come, a man must be prepared to hold his ground and fight his corner. Watch for Brazilian actress Alice Braga in a supporting role here. We hope to see more of her on American screens in the future.

8. Fear X (2003)

A repressed security guard (John Turturro) is searching for answers to who killed his wife. His strange behavior and ticking time-bomb manner begin to alarm friends and co-workers. One day he finds some information that may be a lead to solving the mystery. This discovery sets him on the path to realization. Or does it?

I am a big fan of the films of Nicolas Winding Refn (The *Pusher* trilogy, and *Valhalla Rising*), and this one is perhaps his most penetrating examination of a wounded psyche. It failed commercially when it first appeared, as many viewers were put off by the artistic flourishes and opaque ending. For me, this film is the deepest study of grief and repressed rage ever filmed. All men will be confronted by tragedy, grief, and inexplicable loss during their lives. How we handle it will define who we are. The greatness of this film is that it explores Turturro's claustrophobic, neurotic world in a deeply personal way, and at the same time suggests that he may actually be on to something. This film covers the same philosophical ground as Francis Ford Coppola's *The Conversation*, in that it hints at the ultimate ambiguity of all things.

30. A WORLD CUP LESSON

The 2014 World Cup will not go down favorably in Brazilian collective memory. First there were the grumblings about the excessive money being spent to host the event, and how those monies could have been put to better use for infrastructure and education. Then there was the shattering 7-1 loss to Germany at the Mineirao stadium in Belo Horizonte in the semi-finals on July 8, which triggered something that looked very much like a national trauma. When the Netherlands defeated Brazil in a 3-0 drubbing, it seemed like the time had come for some national soul-searching. It was the first time since 1940 that Brazil had been defeated in consecutive home games. What rankled even more was the fact that arch-rival Argentina made it to the finals with a respectable showing in all of her matches. Something had gone seriously wrong.

The statistics mask the scale of the calamity in the Brazilian psyche. The last time Brazil hosted the World Cup (in 1950), it lost the final to Uruguay by a score of 2-1, with Uruguay scoring its two goals in the last 13 minutes. That defeat caused Brazilian playwright and journalist Nelson Rodrigues to describe the event as "a national catastrophe...our Hiroshima." The analogy is not as hyperbolic as it sounds. Brazil has long defined itself on its virtuosity on the football field; there was a sense that, despite all of her underachievement in other areas of endeavor, there was at least something that Brazil was the best at. The sport provided a national narrative, a somewhat effective social glue, and a sense of pride. According to anthropologist Roberto DaMatta, football gave Brazil "a confidence in ourselves that no other institution has given Brazil to the same extent." Seen against this backdrop, the psychological effect of Brazil's showing in the 2014 World Cup games has been nothing less than devastating.

To be sure, there is a danger in reading too much into the outcomes of sporting events. We must not make the mistake of projecting a whole host of wider "societal lessons" onto a misfortune on the field of play. No sporting team can win all the time, and slumps are natural parts of the competitive cycle. The July 12, 2014 print issue of *The Economist* contains an editorial by a writer named "Bello" which sees Brazil's defeat as a symptom of a "wider malaise" in Brazil's economic and political fabric. Bello claims that the World Cup disaster is likely to rob President Rousseff of a "boost in an election in October" and that "Brazilian football is no longer a source of national confidence." Such statements go too far, I believe. The World Cup soccer field is not a distillation of the Brazilian national experience.

But there is something to be learned here, and something to take away. This is an opportunity to reflect on the virtues of perseverance, resilience, and willpower. We can use Brazil's crushing defeats to make wider points about recovering from major setbacks. No one can coast through life without experiencing traumas and disasters. Defeats can come in personal, financial, or emotional forms. The great god Pain--to use an expression from German writer Ernst Jünger--will place his hand on our heads many times during our lives. How we deal with the effects of his touch will provide some indication of our worth.

Competition is the essence of life itself. It is a biological imperative. Nations and empires are much like individuals, in that they have their own characters and traits. Some have the capacity to adapt and learn from their defeats, and thereby emerge stronger from calamity; and some are unable to change their ways, eventually becoming buried by the winds and dusts of historical events. Nations, like individuals, make their own choices whether to learn from their catastrophic defeats. In my own experience, I have seen some men laid low by defeat, never to recover. Others have learned from their experiences and gone on to greater achievement, fortified by the gauntlet of hardship. Defeat is a stimulus for reform for some, and a death-knell for others.

Historical examples abound. Assyria was one of the most militarily proficient and feared empires of the ancient Near East. It set a benchmark for ruthless cruelty that few predecessors could match. From Egypt to Babylon, it controlled a domain held together by administrative force and fear. One of its great kings, Ashurbanipal, died in 626 B.C.; fourteen years later, a coalition of Scythians, Babylonians, and Medes swept into Nineveh, the Assyrian capital, and sacked it. From this one great blow, Assyria never recovered. It essentially disappeared from history, never to rise again. Its society had failed to establish the rehabilitative institutions, and the cultural depth, that might have provided some relief from a major calamity. Hundreds of years later, when the Greek general Xenophon led his army over the broken ruins of Nineveh, he had no idea that it was once the seat of a great and prosperous empire.

Rome in the Second Punic War provides an illustration of a different result. At the Battle of Cannae in 216 B.C., Rome faced a military disaster of the greatest magnitude. Some 50,000 of its men—more than half her army—were slaughtered by Hannibal's battlefield brilliance. In one day, the cream of the Roman army was ground into the bloody soil of Apulia, among them many senators and members of Rome's most notable families. The scope of the calamity is difficult for us to comprehend today, but it registered in Rome as something like a Hiroshima event. The city lay open, and the public went into a general panic. For the first time, Rome knew the taste of fear.

But this is where Rome showed that it was not Assyria. Rome adjusted her tactics, replaced her leaders, and dug in for a long and protracted fight. With grim determination, it adopted Fabius Maximus's policy of outlasting Hannibal. Deprived of decisive military engagements, Hannibal floundered around Italy for years, losing strength, vainly trying to build a coalition of allies to confront Rome. Rome meanwhile went on the offensive elsewhere, sending Scipio Africanus to attack Carthaginian strongholds in Hannibal's rear in Spain. Slowly but surely, Roman tenacity wore down Carthaginian panache and brilliance. It was a war of attrition, a battle of willpower to see who could outlast the other. Hannibal was finally forced to return home, and at Zama he was decisively defeated by Scipio.

It will be illuminating to see how Brazil responds to its soccer-field Cannae. Will it use this defeat as an impetus to improve and come back stronger? Or will it collapse as did Assyria? Those who know Brazil already know the answer to this question. I am confident that Brazil will emerge stronger, better, and more humble from this experience. In retrospect, it seems that Brazilians approached the games with too much arrogance, too much hubris, and too much laxity.

It is still too early to know the full story, but I suspect that the Germans made a detailed study of their opponents' style of play and weaknesses, and planned patiently for their match with Brazil. This type of meticulous preparation is a hallmark of the German way of doing things. One is reminded of German boxer Max Schmeling's 1936 bout with universal favorite Joe Louis. While everyone predicted Louis would quickly dispose of the upstart German, Schmeling patiently and quietly studied films of Louis's technique in order to dissect his opponent's weaknesses. He found a hole in Louis's defenses, and exploited it. I am sure the German World Cup team here did precisely the same thing against their Brazilian opponents.

No one can shield himself from defeat. It will come whether we want it or not. How we respond to our defeats is the determinative issue. For the laurels go not to the man who begins the race, but to the man who finishes it.

31. THE ART OF SPEAKING AND WRITING WELL

When Rome conquered Greece, it adopted many of her techniques of education. One of these was the emphasis on rhetoric as a field of study, defined as the art of speaking and writing well. Rhetoric became a highly sophisticated subject, and rhetorical training was in great demand in imperial Rome for anyone aspiring to a career in government or politics. Rome had no formal "state prosecutor" system as we do today; individuals needed to bring their own criminal or civil cases before a tribunal (*iudices*) and hire lawyers to argue on their behalf. Historians also were trained rhetoricians; the works of Livy, Tacitus, Sallust, Ammianus Marcellinus, and others are filled with robust speeches and artful epigrams that demonstrate the influence of rhetorical training on these authors as well.

Classical historians viewed history almost as a branch of rhetoric. They filled their volumes with imaginary speeches, deciding for themselves what historical actors "ought" to have said on each occasion. Readers apparently were unperturbed. Modern ideas about historiography had not arrived yet, and the writing of history remained the province of rhetoric, much like science hid in the shadow of philosophy for so many centuries. What mattered to readers more than rigid historical accuracy was a flowing narrative with a moral lesson. To be an effective historian meant to be able to hold a reader's attention and deliver a compelling narrative.

This article will give an overview of some the best rhetorical writings that have survived from this period. The techniques that these old masters described are still valid today. Who among us does not wish to improve his speaking or writing? Who among us does not wish to improve his character? A close study of Cicero, Seneca the Elder, and Quintilian show just how developed classic rhetorical techniques were. I will treat each of these writers individually.

Cicero. Cicero, of course, needs no introduction. The only Roman who surpassed the Greek orators in eloquence and verbal dexterity, his speeches remain masterpieces of declamation, invective, persuasion, and philosophical subtlety. Space here prevents a detailed review of his career and works, but it is sufficient to say that the Catilinian orations, the Verrine orations, and his so-called *Phillipics* still stand today as exemplars of the rhetorical art. Less well known, however, is his short treatise *On the Classification of Rhetoric* (*De Partitione Oratoria*). Although a technical treatise, it contains much of value to the serious student of oratory. According to Cicero, the functions of an orator were: (1) *inventio*, the discovery of arguments meant to influence an audience; (2) *collocatio*, the proper arrangement of arguments in a form suitable to maximize effect; (3) *elocutio*, the differing varieties of speaking styles; (4) *actio*, techniques of delivery; and (4) *memoria*, the cultivation of the memory.

According to Cicero, a speech can be divided into these constituent parts: (1) *exordium*, the introduction, designed to win favor with the audience; (2) *narratio*, the "statement of the case", which should be direct, clear, and uncluttered; (3) *confirmatio*, a laying out of "proofs" by reciting facts or valid precedent; (4) *reprehensio*, a refutation of the opponent's points; and (5) *peroratio*, the all-important summation, in which everything is brought together. Cicero goes into great detail with each of these components of a speech, and the reader senses the hand of a master on every page of the treatise. Although such a taxonomy sounds dry, it is necessary in speech-making to begin with first principles. All of Cicero's speeches follow a very precise format, and one can only appreciate them if one has some idea of what theoretical framework he was guided by.

Seneca The Elder. Not to be confused with his more well-known son Seneca the philosopher, Seneca the Elder was a Spanish rhetorician who, late in his life, collected his lessons from a lifetime of teaching into a comprehensive handbook. Seneca was concerned with two types of speeches: the arguing of legal controversies (*controversiae*) and *suasoriae*, which were speeches on deliberative topics. Students improved their speaking and writing by means of "declamations" (*declamationes*), defined as the giving of imaginary speeches. Seneca had an incredibly detailed memory, cultivated by years of practice in speech-giving. The two volumes of his book contain his recollections of the sayings, advice, and sample exercises of other master rhetoricians. Most of it appears to have been written directly from his prodigious memory.

How did these "declamations" work in practice? The instructor would offer a proposition or legal issue, such as the following:

> A man disinherited his son. The disinherited son went to a prostitute and had a son by her. He then became sick and sent for his father. When his father came, he entrusted his son to his father, and then died. After his death, the father adopted the boy. The man's other son accuses the father of diseased mind (*dementia*).[42]

---

[42] Abdicavit quidam filium; abdicatus se contulit ad meretricem; ex illa sustulit filium. Aeger ad patrem misit; cum venisset, commendavit ei filium suum et decessit. Pater post mortem illius adoptavit puerum; ab altero pater filio accusatur dementiae. [*Controv.* II.4].

Some of the topics of declamation in Seneca's book are bizarre, and apparently were designed to foster creative thinking in pupils. Students would then have to argue the merits and issues of each side, within strict time limits. Their techniques and logic would be critiqued by the instructor, and they would then have to argue the opposite side. Seneca's book is filled with interesting bits and pieces of rhetorical wisdom and amusing anecdotes accumulated from a lifetime in the oratorical trenches. It is surprising that he is so obscure today. But perhaps declamations and oral gymnastics appeal only to lawyers.

Quintilian. The most complete study of the rhetorical art is to be found in Quintilian's *Institutio Oratoria* (The Orator's Education). This work, written in a clear and vigorous Latin, and filling five volumes in the Loeb Library series, is a virtual encyclopedia on proper speaking. Quintilian was the rector of a school of rhetoric, and wrote his masterwork in old age for the intended use of his sons; but tragedy overtook his family, and both his sons died as youths. He poured all his experience, his wisdom, and his repressed anguish into his work. Perhaps we, his readers, are his sons; for on every page we feel the magnetism and rectitude of a strong character backed by an unwavering moral compass. For him, a man cannot be a good speaker without having a sound moral character:

Nothing is so busy, so many-formed, so ravaged and sliced up by so many different affections, as an evil mind. When it is occupied in evil enterprise, it is drawn out with hope, cares, and labor. Even when its crime has been reached, it is racked by solicitude and remorse, and the anticipation of punishment. With all of this, what room is there for literature and cultural life? No more, by God, than there is room for a good crop where the land is full with thorns and overgrowth.[43]

He believed that the aspiring orator should study music and dance to give himself balance and rhythm; athletics to cultivate his physique; literature and philosophy to mold his character and reasoning; and science to sensitize himself to physical reality. Here is a prescription not just to be a good speaker, but to be a good man. He recognizes that his training program is arduous, and has no illusions that most will be up to the task. He (perhaps unfairly) disliked Seneca the philosopher, considering him a wordy pedant, but greatly admired Cicero as the undisputed master of his art. (With regards to Seneca, what may have offended Quintilian was more Seneca's apparent hypocrisy than his rhetoric). Regarding the actual mechanics of giving a speech, Quintilian offers mountains of practical advice. Among the best bits of wisdom are:

1. Do not write your speech down unless you intend to deliver it verbatim, which will rarely happen. It will interfere with the spontaneity of the delivery. Instead, outline it, and know those topics thoroughly.

2. Clarity is the most important virtue of all. A written composition must be set aside for a time, then patiently revised again. A piece of writing that is laid aside, and then approached again, will appear to be almost the writing of another hand. Be ruthless with your pruning, and remember that your listeners will have little patience with verbosity.

3. Avoid wild gesticulations when speaking, but seek the mastery of effective hand movements. Quintilian has an entire

---

[43] *Inst. Ora.* XII.1

section in his treatise on the proper types and employment of hand movements as an aid to communication.

Tacitus and Pliny the Younger are counted among Quintilian's pupils, and they represent some of the best in Latin literature. He was a great influence on St. Augustine and many early Church fathers who received a rhetorical instruction. Nearly forgotten in the Middle Ages, interest in him was revived during the Renaissance when a complete manuscript of the *Institutes* was discovered by Poggio Bracciolini in a monastery in 1416.

All in all, Quintilian embodies the best that classical rhetoric can offer. We feel the immediacy of his message that the training of character is just as important as the importation of knowledge; and his pages resonate with the dignity, humanity, and wit of an experienced schoolmaster. Modern education has done young men a disservice by neglecting the development of virtue and character. One gets the sense, from reading the works of the ancients, that modern methods of instruction have pushed the acquisition of huge volumes of technical information at the expense of the development of character. We are paying dearly for this deficiency. Perhaps the secret of Rome's longevity lies in the fact that its educated elite emphasized character as much as wisdom. Its best and wisest men knew that, without a foundation in character, a man was doomed. Eloquence, for all its luster, eventually loses its shine without a firm footing in worldly virtue. In words that our millennial generation would do well to remember, he cautions us:

The young should not be held back in an artificial world, or become used to inane things to the point where they find it hard to abandon them, lest they become accustomed to such protective shades, and shrink from the bright sunlight of reality.[44]

The best teachers, to be sure, are not only transmitters of knowledge, but are also stimuli for our moral renovation. We have never needed such teachers more than we do now.

---

[44] ...sic adulescentes non debent nimium in falsa rerum imagine detineri et inanibus simulacris usque adeo ut difficilis ab his digressus sit adsuefacere, ne ab illa in qua prope consenuerunt umbra vera discrimina velut quendam solem reformident. [*Inst. Ora.* X.5]

32. FOREIGN LANGUAGE COMPOSITION

Previous articles in these pages have discussed techniques for improving one's speaking, reading, and listening abilities in a foreign language. This focus is understandable, as most language students will have as their primary goal the speedy acquisition of conversational proficiency. Until now, however, little attention has been paid to the area of written proficiency: that is, how to improve one's abilities to write compositions in a foreign language. It is a neglected topic that merits discussion. Writing proficiency is the capstone of language mastery; and the ambitious student will not shy away from accepting this challenge. Sooner or later, there will be occasions when we will need to write, in our target language, a letter, email, resume, a short essay, or some other extended composition.

The arts of composition and translation involve a different set of skills than those required for speaking and listening. Prose composition sharpens the linguistic abilities, focuses our artistic flourishes, and forces us to discipline our wayward grammar. We will discuss some general principles that will provide a foundation for future study.

Composition is the art of rendering a passage from one's native language (for most readers here, English) into the target language. From the start, the student must be guided by attention to the following three things: (1) precision of expression; (2) grammatical accuracy; and (3) grace of style. *Precision of expression* is the ability to write passages that accurately convey the meaning and spirit of the original. *Grammatical accuracy* is fidelity to all the nuances and minutiae of our target language's rules, syntax, and orthography. *Grace of style* is the ability to write a passage that is more than just a clumsy reproduction of the original English. Stylistic elegance is an art attained only by constant practice and exposure to good writings. Ideally, our goal should be to produce a composition that a native speaker might recognize as something linguistically honorable and worthy of his own pen. How to achieve these three elements of good composition? We will discuss each of them in greater detail.

Precision of Expression

Precision of expression is essentially the efficient use of words, phrases, clauses, and sentences to convey the meaning of the original English into the target language. One must develop an instinct of what is correct or preferred usage, and what is not. A helpful technique here is the concept of the *exemplar*: we must seek out paragons of written style in our target language, and imitate this paragon. Imitation is the father of precise expression. A writer works with his target language in the same way that a pizza-maker rolls and stretches his dough: handling skills must first come from imitation of a master, combined with constant practice.

Every language has writers or sources that are generally considered models of good style. Our task is to seek out such exemplars of style, and imitate them, in order to acquire a feel for word order and turn of phrase. We cannot produce good words if we are not reading good words. I would suggest here that students seek out the most respected news and current affairs websites in their target language, and constantly read the short articles or essays found there. The language of the modern media is vital to master. In the modern media will be found the most current words, expressions, cultural references, idioms, and topics of the day. This can be supplemented by reading one or more excellent modern literary authors in the target language.

The student of Brazilian Portuguese, for example, might study and imitate the written styles found in the articles of the website for *O Globo*; the student of Arabic, *Al Jazeera*; the student of Latin, the writings of Caesar, Livy, Celsus, Quintilian, or Augustine, as well as the excellent *Nuntii Latini* website. Every language has such recognized media sites or respected stylistic masters. When reading these articles or passages, we should take particular note of cultural references, common constructions, and idiomatic expressions that cannot be found in textbooks. Our exemplar should produce writing that is lucid, relatively simple, and vigorous.

Prose is preferred to poetry. The language of poetry does not make for good style, and should be avoided. Poets write for aesthetic effect, and their constructions (often employing archaisms and unusual words or word order) do not conform to standard usage. We should also avoid using excessively colloquial usages, as well as very antiquated language. Such things are fine for quotations, but not as models of proper written style. In general, older writers have a more solid, consistent masculine force, in contrast to much of the rather insipid and undisciplined writing encountered today.

Grammatical Accuracy

Grammatical accuracy is a function of two areas: *syntax* (the arrangement of words and phrases in proper order), and *orthography* (correct spelling). Here again, correct grammar can only be acquired by constant exposure to our good exemplars, as noted above. In the beginning stages of composition, it will be necessary to follow (slavishly if necessary) our exemplars in all they do. Once a firm footing has been achieved, we can bring our own "personality" to bear on our compositions. Grammar and construction drills done in language textbooks are a good start here, but they must be followed up by actual exposure to passages from good exemplars.

Grace of Style

Grace of style is perhaps the area in which talent or innate ability has the most leeway. To compose or translate well, one must himself be a good stylist. A good translation stands as a work of art unto itself; and even a mediocre piece of writing may be elevated by a spirited rendition in another language. The *Rubaiyat* of Omar Khayyam, for example, was little known in the West until Edward Fitzgerald's masterful translation of the original Persian brought it to life.

In general, the following common stylistic pitfalls are to be avoided: (1) a monotonous series of short, staccato sentences; (2) repetitious use of the same constructions or words; (3) oafish arrangement of words that might not be pleasing to a native speaker; (4) improperly balanced sentences where one or more subordinate clauses do not properly connect to the main idea of the sentence. A good test of stylistic grace is to read your composition aloud to a native speaker. If he or she winces during your delivery, you will know what needs to be corrected. There are foreign language Internet listservs, chatrooms, and interactive websites where students can find immediate (and brutal) feedback on their writing efforts.

From my own experience, the following points also should be kept in mind:

1. *Beware irregular verbs, metaphors, and idiomatic expressions.* Every language has its own vexatious irregular verbs. Unfortunately for us, the most difficult irregular verbs are usually the most commonly used ones (e.g., verbs of saying, thinking, being, giving, having, going, being able, wanting, putting, coming, bringing, etc.). We must be especially sensitive to such verbs and to their correct employment. Proper use comes only with practice, cultural exposure, and attention to detail.

2. *Do not be afraid of the language.* Use a wide variety of constructions: passive voice, indirect statements, subjunctive moods, etc. Some commenters offer artificial "rules" that say you

should or should not use certain types of constructions (e.g., "avoid the passive voice"). This view is unreasonably narrow-minded, and dulls the expressive beauty of the target language. My personal advice, which I will enjoin, is to dive in, roll around in your language's words and phrases, bathe yourself in them, and use whatever you will. Nearly anything is fair game, as long as it is pleasing to the palate. As Virgil says, we must "repeat, and urge, and repeat again."[45]

3. *Translate thoughts, not exact words*. Any written passage can be seen as both a construct of words, and as a construct of ideas. We must be mindful of the whole, while showing deference to the constituent parts. Before translating a passage, read it through completely to get a sense of its full meaning. Do not try to aim constantly for a literal translation. Our goal should be a translation that is faithful to the original wording, but not just a pale imitation of it. Different languages have quite different ways of expressing the same idea, and we *must not* try to force our target language into accepting the same constructions of our mother tongue.

4. *Beware the computer*. Online translation services like Google Translate, and commercially available software translation services, are more limited than generally supposed. I have nothing against these services *per se*—I use them myself—but we should be mindful of their severe shortcomings. Google Translate simply cannot produce a product that is both grammatically correct and stylistically pleasing. They may be fine for short, simple sentences, but you cannot rely on these computer crutches. I was recently reminded of the limits of the computer when I bought a software dictation package (which I will not name here). It supposedly could render one's spoken words into

---

[45] *Aen.* III.436.

coherent written text. In practice, it was nearly useless, turning out only streams of gibberish. The effort required to fix its output of words could have been used to write them correctly from the beginning, a fact that rendered the software pointless. On the other hand, the Internet has opened up opportunities for Skype-related interactions and tutoring with native speakers. I have no personal experiences with such services, but anecdotal accounts related to me thus far have been positive.

5. *Free yourself from your resources*. Too much reference to your dictionary or grammar books will only deflect your progress. Cut loose from your moorings, and sail freely in these rough waters. No dictionary or grammar book can give you a precise knowledge of what word or phrase to use in a particular circumstance. The best preparation for composition is, as I have already said, the reading of vast amounts of text in your target language. You will never be able to ride your composition bicycle until you remove your training wheels. It is not a legitimate excuse to plead that one does not have the time to master these arts. It is only a matter of will and priorities. Effective study takes far less time than is generally believed, and the rewards far exceed anything that can be generated by idle leisure.

I will say one final word on these matters. We should be mindful of Quintilian's admonition on the importance of good character in speaking and writing well. He sagely counsels us that

No one can be a proper orator unless he speaks with honor, knows honor, and hears honor.[46]

Nothing good, in other words, will flow from our mouth or pen unless we ourselves are good and decent men. This should be our ultimate object. For our writing, as well as our speaking, is a mirror of our soul and of its mortal health.

---

[46] *Inst. Orat.* XII.3.

33. RED EMINENCE:
THE IRON WILL OF CARDINAL RICHELIEU

Of the many leadership traits, willpower has special significance. Difficult to describe, it is best illustrated by historical example, rather than by general discussion. That sustained application of effort over a long period of time, and that concentrated focus on ends in the face of myriad obstacles, are manifested in the life of Armand Jean du Plessis de Richelieu (1585-1642). Cardinal Richelieu was France's most subtle, iron-willed, and ruthless statesman. He was will incarnate, and arguably more than any other, he was the maker of modern France.

From an early age he showed an ability to grasp the essentials of a complicated situation and mold them to his advantage. His maternal grandfather had been a Parisian political figure, and his father, the Seigneur de Richelieu, had been Grand Provost of the Royal Household under Henry IV. In an age when the titles of nobility meant far more than they do today, he made the most of his connections.

His family had him nominated for the position of a bishopric in 1606, but he was only twenty one. The young lad then traveled to Rome and made a direct appeal to Pope Paul V; he charmed the pope by first lying about his age, and then by asking for forgiveness for his lie. Paul, not knowing whether to be angry or pleased, was won over by the audacity and keenness of the French youngster. He here demonstrated that remarkable ability to influence men of power, a skill he was to use to great effect throughout his long career. He discharged his duties as bishop with patient application and a probing intelligence that few of his contemporaries possessed. While others focused on enriching themselves with the spoils of office, Richelieu was more interested in advancement.

He was nominated by his peers in 1614 to serve as delegate to the States-General; and from there it was but a short jump to be made secretary of state two years later with the help of Marie de Medicis (queen consort of Henry IV, and regent for her son Louis XIII). He knew how to make himself indispensable to those holding the reins of power. But he was no mere court sycophant. His intellect and memory were second to none, and he had a quiet tenacity of purpose that preserved the ends, while permitting a remarkable flexibility of means. Frequently underestimated, he frustrated all who crossed swords with him.

His fortunes temporarily fell when one of his allies in court was killed. The Queen Mother was banished along with Richelieu, and she soon joined an opposition faction. Richelieu, at the request of the new powers in court, managed to mediate the dispute between the parties and get her back into the king's favor. Louis awarded him the position of cardinal, and from there he became prime minister in 1624 at the age of thirty nine.

The working relationship of King Louis and Richelieu was so successful because each was aware of, and complemented, the qualities of the other. Too many kings err, Richelieu felt, in not letting themselves be served by their ministers. Although the king was always jealous of Richelieu's abilities, he recognized that he could not do without him. No one else had the will and means to keep the Huguenots in check, the French nobles in their place, and ambitious Spain at bay. Richelieu cared little about theology; his purpose was to make France a powerful, centralized state, and to this end, any means was permitted. He would confound many of his clerical colleagues in Rome by his ability to make alliances equally with Protestant as well as Catholic powers. But for him, the interests of France came first.

The siege of the city of La Rochelle shows Richelieu at his most intrepid. This Huguenot stronghold had become nearly an independent city, a situation no sovereign in Paris could tolerate. Richelieu assumed the role of military commander and, acting on behalf of the king, ordered a blockade of the recalcitrant city. Showing an amazing grasp of siege warfare and engineering problems, he had the harbor sealed, and closed all land approaches to the city. The starving fortress surrendered after thirteen months of misery, and Richelieu entered in triumph on horseback. Yet his peace terms to the Huguenots thereafter were lenient and just. He later explained that "differences in religion never prevented me from rendering to the Huguenots all sorts of good offices." In an age of religious intolerance, it was a revolutionary view.

He also put France's arrogant nobility in its place. France at the time was still very feudal in character; the nobles in the provinces still maintained private armed forces, castles bristling with weapons, and courts of law. These semi-independent potentates could on a whim undermine the central authority in Paris. It was a situation that was impeding France's national development, and Richelieu, with the tacit approval of the king, was determined to bring the aristocracy to heel. In 1626 he issued an order mandating the disarming of all private castles and fortresses, and outlawed the aristocratic diversion of dueling. When two barons defied the ban, Richelieu had them executed. "It is a question of breaking the neck of duels or of your Majesty's edicts", he explained to the king.

Frances's nobles were furious, and plotted his downfall. But he was more adroit then they. The Queen Mother, who had originally promoted Richelieu, made no secret of the fact that she had come to despise his special confidence with the king. She had underestimated her one-time protege, and had woken up to find him running France. She demanded that Louis get rid of the subtle cardinal, who had now become informally known as "his red eminence" (*L'Eminence Rouge*). Richelieu, surprising the Queen

Mother by entering her private chamber from a secret passage, confronted her. What precisely he said (or did) to her is not known. There followed a palace drama that was as startling as it was decisive. The king, not temperamentally suited to showdowns, wavered, and left the palace in distress. Richelieu, in a private audience with Louis, persuaded him of his indispensability. He was so successful in this that Louis ordered his own mother banished, had several rebellious nobles executed, and had Richelieu confirmed once again in power. It was a counter-coup of stunning brilliance.

Richelieu then went on ruthlessly to clip the wings of France's provincial governors and the local *parlements*. "Nothing so upholds the laws," he said when meting out punishments to the nobles, "as the punishment of persons whose rank is as great as their crime." He had made France an authoritarian state, but this was seen by most at the time as an improvement over the feudal oppression and chaos that had haunted France for centuries.

He was a man of austere and pale expression, whose delicate features masked a consuming willpower and tenacity of purpose. In the practice of statecraft and political maneuvering, he was without peer. The famous portrait of him by Philippe de Champaigne (now in the Louvre) shows an almost ascetic figure, a man weary with the exercise of authority. He understood the nature of man, and knew that a sovereign could not rule with pleas to moral ideals. Severity was mostly a virtue in a ruler, he believed, and without it a king would not be on the throne for long. Like all of us, he had his faults. He paid too little attention to France's domestic affairs, he taxed the peasantry to the point of destitution, and he set a precedent for absolutism that would be inherited and abused by those who followed him (most notably Louis XIV).

But above all, his willpower was supreme. Frequently ill, he accomplished nearly all of the king's (or his own) purposes that he set out to do, and left France better than he had found it. He knew of the loneliness of power, and accepted the price paid by those who would wield it. "Great men", he once said, "who are appointed to govern states are like those condemned to torture, with only this difference, that the latter receive the punishment of their crimes, the former of their merits."

It is a judgment that we would be hard pressed to dispute.

34. The Visionary War Photography
of Alexander Gardner

In 1856, a thirty five year old Scotsman named Alexander Gardner arrived in New York City to begin employment as a photographer for Matthew Brady's celebrated portrait studio. Gardner had worked hard all his life in Scotland, having been variously employed as a jeweler, a journalist, and finally as a newspaper editor. But his hobby and passion was science, and in the evenings, he taught himself the rudiments of optics, chemistry, and mathematics. When the new art of photography came into its own in the 1840s and 1850s, it was only natural that Gardner would be drawn to the field, and he soon became as expert as any man could be in its techniques. Matthew Brady was the closest thing America had to an official "court" photographer. He owned galleries in New York and Washington, had won recognition in international exhibitions, and was sought out by the rich and powerful in both America and Europe. Anyone who was anyone in the 1850s wanted to sit for a photograph in one of Brady's studios.

One year after Gardner's arrival in America, Brady asked him to manage his studio in Washington, D.C. The fact that Brady had paid for his passage to New York, and had appointed him to such a position of responsibility so quickly, makes it likely that Brady had discovered him during one of his European trips and had been impressed by the Scotsman's intensity and self-taught knowledge.

When the Civil War broke out in 1861, Brady was able to tap his government connections in Washington to get permission to accompany the Union armies in the field. Bored with the drudgery

191

of static portrait photography, he was excited by the idea of using the new art form to record the events of history as they actually happened. Brady got what he asked for, but there was one unwelcome catch: he would have to pay for his venture himself. No government appropriation yet existed for such an untested enterprise. He was on his own.

War photography was not invented in the American Civil War. Battlefields of the Crimean War (1853-1856) had been photographed, but these were primitive and lifeless products, reflecting the experimental state of the art at the time. But improvements came quickly once Brady and Gardner applied themselves to solving the many technical difficulties presented by taking and developing photographs in the field. They invented a truly mobile photographic laboratory and darkroom, a horse-drawn wagon within which was contained all of the apparatus, chemicals, and equipment of the photographer's art. One wonders what the soldiers of the Army of the Potomac must have made of this strange new contraption which needed to be kept scrupulously light-proof at all times.

Images were exposed using the "wet-plate" method. Under yellow light, Gardner or an assistant would coat a piece of clean glass with a mixture of chemicals called collodion (guncotton dissolved in alcohol and sulfuric ether, to which was added bromide and potassium iodide). The plate would be dried to exactly the right point, and then immersed in silver nitrate. It would then be quickly inserted into a sealed container and rushed to the camera outside the wagon, which had already been positioned on a tripod. Any speck of dust, any particle of dirt, or any slight change in humidity could ruin a plate and void all the labor expended. It was a delicate, unforgiving process, requiring a deft hand and a sustained concentration.

Gardner photographed many of the Eastern battlefields of the war, but parted with Matthew Brady in 1863. Setting up his own gallery in Washington, D.C., he recorded the dramatic events in the immediate aftermath of the war: Lincoln's funeral, the trials of the Lincoln conspirators, and the trial of the infamous Henry Wirz, the commandant of Andersonville Prison, who was executed in 1865 for his brutal treatment of Union prisoners. Gardner left Washington in 1867 to head for the western frontier, and took many memorable photographs there for the Union Pacific Railroad before his untimely death in 1882.[47]

Gardner's unique contribution to the history of war photography appeared in 1866 with the publication of his two-volume *Photographic Sketch Book of the War*. No one had ever seen anything like it before. Each volume contained fifty full-page war photographs that had been taken by Gardner or his assistants; on facing pages were descriptions of the pictures' context and relevance. Properly speaking, these were not "combat photographs" in the sense of having been taken during the actual fighting; they were post-combat pictures intended to show the devastation that resulted from modern war.

In Gardner's day, there did not yet exist reliable techniques of mass producing photographic negatives for book publishing. What printers usually did was to hire an illustrator to make a lithograph, drawing, or engraving from an original photo, and then set this copy into a newspaper, magazine, or book. Gardner, ever the photographic purist, felt that this technique would diminish the visual impact of his war photos. So he made a daring and visionary decision: he would make his *Sketch Book* a collection of actual photographic positives, each photograph pasted carefully into its proper page.

---

[47] Gardner's work on the American frontier forms an impressive body of work in its own right. Its positive focus on the nation's expansion and construction forms a contrast to the destruction of the Civil War.

The idea was audacious, expensive, and a commercial failure. Because of the unique way the *Sketch Book* was prepared, the two volume set sold for a price of $150, which was a huge sum for a book in the 1860s. Sales were poor. The prohibitive price, and a general feeling of war fatigue in the public, meant that Gardner's revolutionary book received very little attention. It is estimated that only two hundred sets were printed, and for this reason it is today extremely rare. Inexpensive reprints began to appear in the 1950s, and these brought Gardner's groundbreaking work to greater appreciation after decades of undeserved obscurity.

What are we to make of these photographs? In Gardner's blasted buildings, shattered bridges, and open-mouthed corpses twisted in the agonies of death, we are immediately made aware of war's reality. There is something disturbing in seeing a bullet-ridden farmhouse set against a scene of forests and pastures, and Gardner had a talent for such juxtapositions. Siege works, mortars, and field guns are lovingly studied by his camera, only to be followed by stark images of the effects of these weapons of war. Gardner may not have invented war photography, but under his hand the art form reached a depth and maturity that has rarely, if ever, been equaled.

Among many haunting passages, the following particularly resonate. Opposite a picture of skeletons excavated at the battlefield of Cold Harbor, he writes:

> Among the unburied on the Bull Run field, a singular discovery was made, which might have led to the identification of the remains of a soldier. An orderly turning over a skull upon the ground, heard something within it rattle, and reaching for the supposed bullet, found a glass eye.

Opposite a photo of bloated and bootless Gettysburg dead, Gardner writes:

Some lay stretched on their backs, as if friendly hands had prepared them for burial. Some were still resting on one knee, their hands grasping their muskets. In some instances the cartridge remained between the teeth, or the musket was held in one hand, and the other was uplifted as though to ward a blow, or appealing to heaven. The faces of all were pale, as though cut in marble, and as the wind swept across the battle-field it waved the hair, and gave the bodies such an appearance of life that a spectator could hardly help thinking they were about to rise to continue the fight.

Twentieth century combat photography has perhaps dulled our appreciation of Gardner's meditative and somber style. We now expect to be in the thick of the action as it happens. While this "real-time" technique has its undeniable merits, there is something to be said for a photograph taken immediately after a military engagement. Carnage is best expressed with a measure of reflection. Unlike real-time combat photography, Gardner's photos are artistic compositions, planned out in minute detail.

There is a quiet, meditative power in these photos, in these panoramas of ruin, these abandoned earthworks, and in these bearded men with melancholy faces leaning up against blasted buildings. They impart a stillness, an awe in the soul, that is not easily shaken off. Gardner's work was so far ahead of its time that his contemporaries lost sight of him. He stands as America's prophet of total war, a harbinger of the earth-shaking violence that would convulse the world in the century to come.

35. The Gap Between Theory And Practice

There is a gulf between theory and practice. It can be a simple matter to know how to do something, but actually doing it may be another matter entirely. We try to adjust ourselves to this tension as best we can, and trudge forward. There will always be some degree of difference between what we say, and what we do. The matter is one of degree. When the gap becomes too wide, we fall into the widening sinkhole of hypocrisy. But where does one draw the line? At what point does the label "hypocrite" become deserved? It is an interesting moral question. The life and career of the philosopher Lucius Annaeus Seneca may provide us with some answers.

Seneca remains a controversial figure. He hailed the virtues of a simple life, yet collected mansions and mountains of money. He advised the quiet of the country, yet lived for the intrigue of the palace. He advised sexual restraint, yet took full advantage of his position for his extramarital gratification. He praised honesty and sincerity, yet flattered the emperor Nero and his cronies as often as he could. To this balance sheet we must add his many positive traits: he did his best to mitigate Nero's worst excesses, he was generous with his friends, he had the courage eventually to resist the tyrant emperor, and he had a first-rate mind. Clearly, Seneca was no angel. But what was he, precisely? The best way of exposing the contradictions in his character are to present his best qualities first, and then describe his less savory ones. We will then discuss what may be concluded.

He was born at Corduba (modern Cordova, Spain) around 4 B.C. His father, a noted rhetor, saw to it that the boy received the finest education possible. He practiced law in Rome, and served a minor office as *quaestor* around 33 B.C. A timely inheritance from his father enabled him to pursue writing and palace politics in Rome. He tutored the young regent Nero for five years, and turned out moral essays (*On Anger, On the Brevity of Life, On Benefits*, etc.) that are beautiful distillations of Stoic thought. But being in proximity to a tyrant was ultimately an impossible position. Slowly he became a prisoner of the palace, unable to do much good, and unable to leave. He begged Nero to let him resign, but the tyrant would not permit it.

He was able to do some good. He donated a significant percentage of his fortune to the imperial treasury to help rebuild Rome after the great fire of 64 A.D. Yet he could not escape the paranoia of his sovereign. Nero accused him of complicity in a plot to dethrone him, and ordered him to take his own life. This he did with quiet dignity. His beloved wife Paulina tried to follow him, but Nero forcibly prevented her suicide.

His writings and letters are masterpieces of the Stoic creed. Wisdom should be the art of living, a skill to be practiced daily. He points out the ideal road, but does not demand it; he is too practical to advocate perfection. There is more wisdom in a handful of his epigrams than in the reams of nonsense penned by many modern writers. Yet the picture is not quite complete. Even sages have dark sides, and Seneca was no exception. He was exiled to Corsica early in his life for scandalous relations with the daughter of a powerful Roman general named Germanicus. His letters from exile, like those of Ovid from his own exile near the Black Sea, do not show him at his stoic best.

He took full advantage of his position to enrich himself. He lent money at crushing rates of interest, and counted his fortune at about three hundred million sesterces (at least five hundred million modern US dollars). He had numerous country estates, while never tiring of denouncing luxury. He posed to scorn imperial courtiers, while occupying a key position as premier.

Accusations of sexual impropriety seemed to follow him wherever he went, leaving us to wonder if there must have been some truth to them. All in all, it is hard to square the beauty of his writings with the realities of his life. What are to think of a man who could write the following, while at the same time maintaining himself in enervating opulence:

> An atrium full of antique marble busts does not indicate nobility. No one in the past has lived for our glory. And neither does what preceded us belong to us. Only the soul makes for nobility, which may rise from whatever condition above Fortune. [*Epistulae* 44.5].

All men are figures of contradiction. It is only a matter of degree. Those who seek and serve power inevitably find themselves forced to make daily compromises that erode their ideals. Undoubtedly, Seneca falls short of his philosophic aspirations. Yet which of us can claim to be any better? Serving a tyrant is an exercise in futility, and he probably sensed he was a marked man no matter what he did. Seneca never claimed to be perfect; he only points the road to virtue. Despite his flaws, there is something endearing about this sly old figure. We recognize ourselves in him, and forgive him his faults. His death and his writings redeemed him for posterity, and washed away the memory of his avarice and pride.

One gets the sense that Seneca was acutely aware of the divergence between what he wrote and how he lived. I imagine that all men who occupy positions of power feel some inner conflict. To translate high ideals into practice: is this not the most difficult thing in history? How many leaders have been able to do this? More than anything else, he is a tragic figure. He was caught between two tensions: the desire for power and wealth, and the desire to live according to Stoic doctrine. He was tormented by his inability to reconcile these two conflicting impulses.

Perhaps this is why he, despite his paganism, was such a revered figure to early Christian writers. Tertullian and St. Augustine practically considered him one of their own, calling him "our Seneca." His writings (if not his example) molded some of the greatest statesman and minds of later centuries. His experiences remind us that life is not black and white. The gap between theory and practice is only made bearable by our sincere effort to bridge the intervening space. And if we accept man as he is, and not as he ought to be, then we must love Seneca.

EPILOGUE

In the summer of 2014 I visited a small used bookstore near the downtown of a large city in the American midwest. Not finding anything to my liking, I finally saw an overlooked stack piled near the store's exit. The owner had just dumped them there, not bothering to sort and shelve them. In it were two volumes that caught my attention. One was Joseph Conrad's *Youth: A Narrative and Two Other Stories*, and the other was D.H. Lawrence's *Women in Love*. I had never heard of the stories in the Conrad title (except *Heart of Darkness*), and there was something about the book itself that made me pause. It was old, and yet solidly made. It had been printed in 1959, and the former owner had given its stiff paperback cover a translucent plastic covering that was now a distinguished yellow. There was an elegant photograph of Conrad on the front cover. *Women In Love* I had hoped to read for some time, but had always found an excuse to put it off. Each book was one dollar.

Youth: A Narrative was a story that made an impression on me. Five old veterans of the merchant service are sitting around a table and telling sea-stories. One of the men, named Marlow, describes his first voyage to the Eastern waters of the world about twenty years earlier. A ship sets out from England to Thailand to deliver a load of coal. The vessel is captained by a man in his first command at sea. Passing through the North Sea, the ship is caught in a serious gale which nearly capsizes her; and she is forced to return to port for an extensive refitting. The narrator notices that rats desert the ship, and seamen, being a suspicious bunch, interpret this as a bad omen. A new crew must be found in

Liverpool. The ship (named *Judea*) finally gets underway, and makes progress across the globe, but disaster hits again near Australia. In the heat of the tropics, the cargo of coal catches fire, and the crew are unable to douse it. Flammable gases in the hold ignite, causing a tremendous explosion, and Marlow is nearly killed in the ensuing chaos.

The crew encounter another ship, named the *Somerville*, and arrange for the *Judea* to be towed into the nearest port in Batavia. But even this goes wrong, as the movement of the ship fans the smoldering coals once again, and the ship takes light. Nothing is to be done except to salvage the remaining gear from the *Judea*; the captain has decided to abandon the burned-out vessel, and divide the crew into three smaller boats, one of which Marlow commands. The crew eventually make it safely to Java, and find their way back to England by steamship. And here Conrad concludes the tale.

To anyone who first experienced the Far East as a young man, this story may resonate. It did with me. It is a mood piece, and the mood is the celebration of youth. Or, more particularly, the celebration of youth crossed by danger in the East. Near the end of his tale, Conrad has Marlow say:

> I have seen the mysterious shores, the still water, the lands of brown nations, where a stealthy Nemesis lies in wait, pursues, overtakes so man of the conquering race, who are proud of their wisdom, of their knowledge, of their strength. But for me all the wisdom of the East is contained in that vision of my youth. It is all in that moment when I opened my young eyes on it. I came upon it from a tussle with the sea—and I was young— and I saw it looking at me. And this is all that it left of it! Only a moment; a moment of strength, of romance, of glamour—of youth!

There is something inexplicably profound in encountering physical hardship and foreign travel as a young man. Those formative trials stay with us, bubbling beneath the surface of our skins, giving us the seasoned complexion that we wear for years thereafter. How we flung ourselves into the cauldrons of Fate! We are the sum total of our experiences, and yet those of our youth seem to stand out in sharper focus when we trace the receding lines of memory in a backward trajectory. The travel, the East, and the danger of those years fuse into one shining ingot, one shining alloy of remembrance. Gone from memory are the unhappy hours we spent in toil and tedium, the hours of hardship and cruelty. There remains only the taste of youth's innocent joys, the harassments of happy sleeplessness, the taste of danger's salt spray about our faces, and the bonds of comradeship. Memory is the ultimate redeemer.

THANK YOU, PATIENT READER.

Made in United States
Troutdale, OR
12/29/2023